North
Tennessee 37203
256-3882
-256-3885 fax
www.educati...en.org
wom...

AIDS Memoir
Journal of an HIV-Positive Mother

Catherine Wyatt-Morley

Kumarian Press

Production supervised by Jenna Dixon
Copyedited by Linda Lotz   *Typeset by CompuDesign*
Text design by Jenna Dixon   *Proofread by Beth Richards*

The text of this book is set in 10/13 Adobe Sabon.
The display type is Lennart Hansson's RunaSerif.
The poetry is set in Agfa Rotis SemiSerif.

Printed in Canada on acid-free paper by Best Book Manufacturers.
Text printed with vegetable-based ink.

Library of Congress Cataloging-in-Publication Data
Wyatt-Morley, Catherine, 1958–   .
    AIDS memoir : journal of an HIV-positive mother / by Catherine
Wyatt-Morley.
        p.   cm.
    ISBN 1-56549-067-3 (pbk. : alk. paper)
    1. Wyatt-Morley, Catherine. 1958—Health. 2. AIDS (Disease)—
Patients—United States—Biography. 3. Mothers—United States—
Biography. I. Title.
RC607.A26W93   1997
362.1'969792'0092—dc21
    [B]   97-253

---

06 05 04 03 02 01 00 99 98 97   10 9 8 7 6 5 4 3 2
                        1st Printing 1997

■ Dedication ■

MY DEAREST CHILDREN,

I want to express my warmest devotion to you, my children, for all the understanding you have shown while I spent countless hours writing. I love you very much with each word I write. You are the first and last thought I have with everything I do.

My beautiful Jalyon, you are so bright, strong, caring and give so much to others. Your volunteering at many HIV/AIDS organizations, conferences, food pantries and AIDS walks has made me very proud of you. Keep your head up and be proud of who you are. Life is not always easy or fair, but you have the courage to fight for what you believe in. Fighting for your beliefs, you will find, becomes very important as life progresses. Don't stop fighting for what's right, that which is found in your heart. Make something good happen for yourself. Believe in yourself. If what you focus on remains positive, hold it close and work daily to accomplish all your dreams. Results don't come easily without courageous effort.

Aaron, my special one. Your kindness and love for people will take you places. I will always hold a special place for you in my heart, and will remember the special times we share together, just talking. The closeness you and I have will never be replaced. Your love of life and people will give you the encouragement and wisdom to move forward. Go with love, God will protect you.

Brandon, my firstborn. You are so intelligent and capable of much. Your knowledge will become great someday. You can become whatever you want, so don't stop trying. I see greatness in you. You have a gift, and I welcome your use of it. I love each wonderful moment we share.

Motherhood has been the biggest challenge of my life. Throughout these years, many things have happened that you have not understood. I hope these entries will help you understand better. I wish to share with you things that are difficult to talk about, not only illness, but also the power of love that is greater than illness and even greater than death. Time is no longer on my side, and there is so much you, my children, need to know. You need to know the greatness I see in each of you, the potential of giving so much to life. You are the future I no longer have, and the symbol of my life and love. Children, my essence lies within these pages, my undying legacy to you. Let me teach you what I know. Children of an HIV-positive mother, you have been chosen to carry on. With strong conviction and generational wisdom, I give you the glory you most often deserve but most never get. Brandon, Aaron, Jalyon, you are the future. In you, you will find my essence.

Years have been spent writing to survive, to remain sane. Writing to you, I stayed focused on you. I am glad I'm blessed with your presence in my life.

For every family in the world facing HIV/AIDS, I share this with you. ■

▪ Contents ▪

▪ Foreword ▪

Susan Ford Wiltshire

CATHERINE WYATT-MORLEY MOVES WITH THE EASY GRACE of the dancer she trained to be. Her smile lights a room. Her appetite for learning is voracious, and when she gets an idea, some version of it will probably come to pass. Her tenacity as a mother is fearsome, her tenderness gentle as feathers. She looks outrage straight in the face, knows and names moral failure when she sees it and never walks out from under the faith and friendships that sustain her. Catherine Wyatt-Morley — middle-class, middle-aged, suburban mother of three — is also HIV-positive, infected by her husband with the virus that causes AIDS.

What follows is her story, a complex interweaving of many stories, as any life fully told must be. Wyatt-Morley's passions are transparent in her writing. They have to do with telling the truth, learning and facing the facts, reaching out to others, and caring for family. She has no truck with hypocrisy or even the hurtfulness closely filled with ignorance. She does not fail to note, for example, that of the many charitable collections organized at her workplace, none was ever taken up for families facing AIDS.

Wyatt-Morley has an uncanny knack for identifying corners of the population where attention to AIDS seldom or insufficiently reaches: women in prison, for example, and vulnerable men and woman among the elderly. She is so determined to reach out to other women, especially minority women (she herself is African American), that she conceived the idea of making a professional video for woman and families facing AIDS, a film that also deals

SUSAN FORD WILTSHIRE is professor of classics at Vanderbilt University. She is the author of *Seasons of Grief and Grace: A Sister's Story of AIDS* and other books. Her *Greece, Rome, and the Bill of Rights* won the Alex Haley Memorial Award for Literary Distinction.

with treatment by health care professionals. Starting with no knowledge of how to do such a thing, and no money with which to do it, she completed the project within eleven months.

In these pages, she addresses the multitude of issues that anyone who is HIV-positive must confront: getting the best information and the proper treatment from doctors; political currents, prejudices, and policies around AIDS; attitudes of the churches; discrimination in the workplace. She also pursues the particular dilemmas of women who are facing AIDS. Should HIV-positive women who have gone through menopause or had hysterectomies take replacement hormones? For those who are mothers, how can family life be maintained and children reassured?

Included here are accounts of how she told the heart-stopping news to her children, and how they responded and continue to respond. She demonstrates that the care taken in the telling is part of the healing and strengthening of families.

Catherine Wyatt-Morley lives out of the truth that the virus that redefined her life does not control her life. She controls her life. Her inquisitive mind has led her to learn everything she can about AIDS-related illnesses and treatments, including those offered by nontraditional medicine, so that she can be a better teacher of others as well as a better caretaker of herself. Her remarkable organizational abilities have led to her membership in a number of AIDS-related groups on the state and national levels. Her deep spirituality enables her to draw strength from poetry, beauty, friendship, and a sense of divine presence in her life. She reminds us all that we are never alone and that, as she writes, "to acknowledge love is to increase the capacity to heal."

This is a book that can help any woman or family facing chronic or catastrophic illness, especially when young children are present. It is a book to be read and to be given to friends. If some of those friends are not readers, read it to them or tell them what it says. It is a book to be celebrated, an enduring testament not just to survival but to the flourishing of the spirit, braced with grit, that enables human beings to live well and help others live well in the face of inestimable odds. ■

▦ Foreword ▦

Karen B. Stevenson

And who knoweth whether thou art come to the kingdom for
such a time as this? —*Esther 4:14*

THE STORM CLOUDS GATHER OMINOUSLY, OBSCURING
the brightly shining sun as it overlooks the horizon. The menacing
sound of thunder rumbles through the tension-filled air, as the
opposing armies march silently toward the battlefield. The stage
has been set and the battle lines drawn. The war for the hearts and
souls of our children has begun. Humankind is engaged in a great
conflict; a war of ideals and values.

Our creator placed a moral compass within each of us. Each of
us knows the difference between good and evil, right and wrong,
our fleshly desires and the spiritual high ground. Yet our struggle
with these elements is always with us. The battleground is our
mind. Love, compassion, joy and hope struggle against hatred,
strife, fear and injustice. Courageous soldiers are needed, but in
these perilous times, many choose to turn away. They choose not
to see the wounded and the dying, not to hear the cries of those
who are suffering, not to heed the call to take up arms against the
twin evils of indifference and ignorance.

Catherine Wyatt-Morley is one who heard the call and answered
it. Moved by the cries of those in pain, although wounded herself,
she did not allow the specter of HIV to bring her down. Instead, she

KAREN B. STEVENSON is a psychiatrist with specialized training in
child and adolescent psychiatry. She spent four years as a captain in the
U.S. Army and is now a major in the U.S. Army Reserves. An African
American, she lives in Nashville with her husband, Roderick, a transplant
surgeon, and their four children. She has dedicated her life to promoting
the idea that each of us has been created for a special purpose and that
each life has infinite value.

rose up to fight the injustice and intolerance that surrounded her. Her own suffering moved her to speak out for those who had not the words to speak for themselves. Her personal anguish has led her to educate a world steeped in ignorance about daily living with HIV.

Catherine produced a video to give us a glimpse into the lives of ordinary people facing an extraordinary struggle. On my recent journey to Ghana, West Africa, I had the privilege of sharing the video with the ministry of Today's Choices–Ghana, which reaches out to women dealing with crisis pregnancies and educates thousands to make responsible and godly choices regarding their sexuality. This video provides a link for all suffering humanity as it reveals our connection to one another.

In her journal and in powerful letters to her children, Brandon, Aaron and Jalyon, Catherine shares a life dedicated to the task of stopping this senseless waste of precious lives. She realizes that our children's lives are in jeopardy and that the stakes are high.

Our children are constantly bombarded with glamorized images of wanton, irresponsible sexuality and are then lured to a false sense of security by the impression that there are easily available and painless remedies for sexual irresponsibility. But then they find that this path in reality leads to a morass of sexually transmitted diseases, unplanned pregnancies, abortions and HIV/AIDS, as well as broken hearts, broken dreams and broken lives.

These perilous times demand that courageous people speak the truth, but temper it with love and compassion. They must expose moral decay and relativism, but infuse their message with hope for a better future. Catherine's vision for a brighter world for her children, and for a society that demonstrates tolerance and compassion toward the hurting, has led her to bare her soul. In her words there is hope and healing.

Catherine Wyatt-Morley, a woman living the American dream, with a beautiful family, a successful career, and a comfortable life in a prestigious suburb, found herself drafted into a powerful army. Mother, activist, educator and friend, Catherine is in the front line in the war for spiritual as well as physical health. She was indeed chosen for the kingdom at such a time as this. God has taken her pain and transformed it into power, and the voice of the victim has been changed to one of victory. ■

■ Preface ■

GROWING UP IN THE 1960S WAS A TIME OF ROCK AND roll, Afros, peace signs and black power. My parents worked, and we were a middle-class family. My mother managed to keep a close eye on me even though she worked full time at the county hospital, where she was supervisor of the dietary, or food service, department.

The younger of two children and the only girl, I grew up very close to two of my cousins, and we often spent nights at one another's houses. There were many happy times at family parties, picnics and gatherings. I learned at a young age the importance of family. At seventeen I graduated from high school and started college the following month. After college, I traveled.

Later, I met Tim and fell in love for the first time in my life. We did everything together, and I was happy. Together we built a wonderful life for ourselves and the three children. Our marriage had its problems, like most marriages, but things always seemed to work themselves out. We moved to Tennessee in 1990 and began wonderful jobs at a manufacturing plant. Eventually, Tim's alcoholism began to play a bigger part in our lives. After several separations, I forgave him for affairs, drugs, and physical abuse, hoping that the five of us could find life together again.

And so we come to today. At age thirty-six, I found out that I was HIV-positive.

My heart is heavy, because it has taken so long to come such a short distance, but as HIV continues to grow within me, I continue to learn — as do the professionals. There is no time for standing still.

I share this personal background not to evoke sympathy but because I have found few resources that examine the struggle of living with HIV/AIDS through the eyes of a mother, wife, daughter, sister, woman of color and faith. Before our diagnosis, the future was a horizon of hope and open-ended possibilities. Relationships with family and friends seemed broad, if not limitless. The present has also taken on a new significance. No longer do I view it as a gateway to the future; rather, the present, along with memories of the past, is all we truly have. Living responsibly in the present is important, and it has new significance for me.

But for others, who have not yet been touched by HIV/AIDS or other chronic ills, the present may not have quite the same urgency and may not hold such an understanding heart. For me, a new personal relationship through faith replaces a quest for understanding. ■

▪ Acknowledgments ▪

TO MY FRIEND KAREN MOORE, I OFFER THANKS FOR listening to my many concerns about this and the many other projects I have undertaken. Susan Wiltshire, Carrie Wiltshire, Deidre Williams, Mark Jackson, Joan Schleicher, Maxine Littleton, Brooke Lambard, Fran Hooten, LaVonna Lender, Cumberland Institute and many others, I thank you for believing in me and my work. Your encouragement will always be remembered. The kindness of all my extended family has given me hope during the storms of my life. All my friends in WOMEN and WORTH have provided much-needed support and encouragement through difficult times of sickness and joy.

Joan Solomon, my development editor, home-schools three children, but she devoted hours to helping me get my efforts into publishable form. Joan would remind me how important my writings are and would say, "I am learning a lot from you." Sherry McMillan, a poet, contacted me after she and her daughter viewed my video "Reasons to Live." Sherry is HIV-negative, but her gift of the poem "I am AIDS," which appears at the beginning of the 1994 section of the book, deeply expresses her concern. She told me that if AIDS could talk, this is what it would say.

For my two special friends, Dr. George Lemon and Mrs. Bernice Lemon, RN, who befriended me, a stranger, at the dentist's office and put me in touch with Kumarian Press, I return your gifts with love. The Lemons believed so strongly in "Reasons to Live: Women, Their Families and HIV," that they presented it three times at the international conference center in Caux, Switzerland.

My heart is softened with the presence of Dr. Ian Mayo-Smith. He and his wonderful wife, Krishna Sondhi, opened their home to me. Krishna and Ian's encouragement moved me toward the great undertaking of publishing this work. Ian wrote the poems "This feeling of despair" (in the entry for August 30, 1995) and "The long walk in the dark" (at the beginning of the 1996 section), as well as the afterword. Throughout the years, Ian has dedicated himself to many worthwhile causes, working with the United Nations Development Programme, Hope in the Cities, the Ford Foundation and MRA Initiatives for Change. His devotion to this book still brings me to tears. Also at Kumarian Press, my thanks go to Trish Reynolds and all the others who helped this first-time author in many ways. Craig Wilkinson of the National Association of People with AIDS has been there for me with practical help and encouragement.

I have been truly blessed with the friendship of all these people who have shared my concerns and my commitment to inform and educate people about HIV and AIDS.

It is important to acknowledge that Roxanne Fyke, who is mentioned in this book (see the entry for December 10, 1995) and who appeared in "Reasons," died in September 1996 and leaves behind two wonderful sons to face life without their mom. Roxanne will be missed by many. I extend compassion to every family in the world facing HIV and AIDS.

As I move forward producing my second video, titled "Policy and People: HIV/AIDS Realities," I pray for blessings to be given to those whose lives will be touched. HIV is a plague in our society. We must stop the cycle of stigmas associated with this disease and open the minds of our children. ∎

▪ Introduction ▪

AIDS MEMOIR: JOURNAL OF AN HIV-POSITIVE MOTHER is a life-lived story, told from my perspective. It describes the events that we lived through while learning about and living with HIV/AIDS. Whenever possible, I have maintained original names, but some names have been changed to give privacy to those whose lives have been intertwined with mine.

I began keeping entries for my children soon after I was diagnosed, because I believed that I would soon die and leave them. Somehow, the writing has sustained me. As I wrote, I began to realize that this story was not ultimately mine to keep for my children. It is a story that should be shared with other families living with illness and HIV/AIDS — other women with children, caregivers, husbands, fathers, mothers, and older persons in search of serenity despite AIDS. So I kept my entries current and wrote accurately as often as I could.

I chose to add some events about personal family situations to allow for deeper understanding. However, other personal writings will remain between me and my children.

The most difficult part of writing this journal has been not knowing how or when to end. When I would think that I should stop writing, some other significant event would unfold, and the fear that the end would be written for me, in another's hand, was always with me. Thoughts of life-threatening, opportunistic infection hung in the room when I wrote. At times, I wondered if I would feel well enough to get back to the computer.

Like most mothers, I prefer a story that is clear, direct and easily understood. I hope that every person reading these pages along with my children will learn something or at least give thought to the words within.

In the beginning, I believed that my entries would stop upon my death, or Tim's death, but I am still alive, and even though much

of what I have written is being published in this book, I now know
that my writings will continue until I can no longer write to my
beautiful children.

Throughout the years of writing, there was always something
to share: a thought, a truth, a poem. When I realized that dying of
AIDS would pale in comparison to living with HIV/AIDS, my
entries began to change. My experience of living with HIV/AIDS
changed my writings. I began to transform as a person as a result
of my experiences living with HIV/AIDS. I am grateful that I have
maintained the health and presence of mind necessary to write.
This journal has given me the determination to continue to tell
my children what it's like to live each moment of one's life with
this illness. ∎

1994

I am AIDS.
Perhaps you've heard of me
For I have infiltrated
Hollywood's movers and shakers.
I have preyed upon
Mothers,
Babies
And children.
I have taken and taken
And will continue to take
All that I perceive as mine
With no thought
To those who are left
To remember
Better times.
For if I have my way
You will only remember
The face of death
And the time and suffering
It took
To be realized.
Yet with all I take,
With every evil I commit
You, self-righteous,
Indulgent,
Sanctimonious ones
Do more harm,
Commit more evil

1

Than any plague will ever do.
Those touched by me
Or any of my co-conspirators
Are the lucky ones,
For their suffering will cease
Eventually.
But for those
Who remain in your society,
You are the ones destined for pain,
As you utter
Insincere condolences
And fault those
Who have them coming.
Your ignorance is your reality,
Shame is your chosen
Tool of destruction.
I bring no one to Lucifer
For he is loose
And among you at your thickest,
You lost ones
Who profess
To be delivered.

Sherry W. McMillan

March 28, 1994   The waiting room at Baptist Hospital was full of magazines tossed around on the impersonal chairs and benches. The patient intake department was decorated in pastel colors, with pictures of abstract objects and matching lamps. I had just sat down and begun adjusting myself for what I believed would be a long wait when I was called by the attending nurse. While she drew my blood, we filled out forms and discussed my anesthesiologist. I hope he's good, because I have things to do when this hysterectomy is over.

March 30, 1994   Tim and I arrived at the hospital at 5:00 A.M. We were led to my room, where I was told to put on a hospital gown and get comfortable in bed. Nervously, I changed and got into bed. Tim stood staring out the window. With his back to me, he told me, "Don't worry, baby, everything'll be fine. We have a trip to plan, remember." I just wanted the hysterectomy to be over and done with.

Soon a nurse and the floor supervisor came in and began to go over the information I had provided. The nurse gave me a shot in the IV she had already hung. It was full of a routine saline solution given to all patients having surgery. The shot was to relax me. Tim and I were told that I was scheduled for a 10:00 A.M. surgery and that the doctors would be arriving at any moment. They said that I would be taken to the pre-op floor soon. I began to relax and feel the heaviness of the medication. Tim stood at the side of the bed looking down at me with loving eyes. "The kids and I love you, Catherine. When you wake up, I will have gotten the kids from school, and we will be waiting to see you." He kissed me as they wheeled my bed toward the double doors of pre-op.

April 1, 1994   Tim brought me home, and I went straight to bed. The children were happy to have Mom home, but I was barely aware of where I was. I was not feeling well at all.

April 2, 1994   I didn't know that I would have this body brace. I've been cut from hipbone to hipbone. What's going on?

April 3, 1994 / Easter Sunday   Early this morning I cried out in pain to Tim. He rushed me to Southern Hills Hospital, where I was immediately admitted. I could not understand what was wrong and why I was feeling so bad. Dr. Thomas Woolridge, our family doctor, was called by the hospital admissions staff. Dr. Woolridge came to see me. He told me that the surgeon had discovered a problem with my blood before the surgery. "Problem, what problem?" I asked. He tried to reassure me that it was nothing serious but that I needed further testing. The nurse came to draw blood.

April 5, 1994   Home from the hospital.

April 12, 1994   When I saw the surgeon this morning for a follow-up visit, he was noticeably standoffish. I could not understand how he could examine me from across the room wearing plastic gloves and a face mask. He admonished me to be sure to keep my appointment with the OB-GYN. I assured him that I would. I told him that I felt awful and the pain was still intense.

"When do you see Dr. Richard?"

"Today at 2:00," I said.

"You're not driving, are you?"

"No, doctor, my husband is in the waiting room, he will drive me. The pain is much too great for me to drive."

The appointment was for 2:00 P.M. Tim and I sat for a long time in the very crowded waiting room, until finally we decided to leave because Aaron had soccer practice at 4:00. By this time, I was feeling weak, and the pain in my abdomen was so intense that my skin felt as if it were on fire. Tim went to tell the receptionist that we were leaving because I was tired and in pain. She went to tell the doctor. He came out and said, "No, you can't leave. I'll be right with you. Please wait in my office."

Tim helped me into the large leather-covered chair across from the doctor's desk. He sat next to me, looking at me with worry.

The doctor entered the room and sat behind his desk. Dr. Floyd Richard, the gynecologist who had been present during the hysterectomy, told Tim and me that I had tested positive for the human immunodeficiency virus — The virus that causes AIDS. "Catherine," he said, "we gave you the ELISA test and the Western Blot test. It looks as if you need to be retested for HIV, the virus that causes AIDS." Tim and I had never heard of these tests. I began to feel nauseated and told the doctor that he had to be mistaken. I had not agreed to being tested before, during, or after the surgery and had not given consent for any such tests. Why was I tested? Who tested me? Finally, I said, " What do we do now?" My head began to swim with fear. Tears filled my eyes. They ran like water from a spout. My body shook, and I held my abdomen as the pain of the hysterectomy reminded me that I was not well.

"But doctor, there have been no signs, no symptoms, no warning. I'm married and have been faithful to Tim," I said, as I looked at my husband, whose beautiful brown eyes were filling with tears. "I have not shot any drugs. I don't understand. I don't know anything about HIV."

My thoughts began to turn to my children. Suddenly, I was afraid for my babies. Oh my God, I am dying.

Tim and I never considered the possibility of being tested for HIV/AIDS. Dr. Richard told us what should happen next. "Catherine, we wait a few weeks and run the test again." Tim said that it seemed logical for him to be tested. The doctor agreed and immediately scheduled his test for the same day. "I am sorry, Catherine," the doctor said. I looked at him and said nothing. Tim and I left his office in utter silence, walking slowly to the parking lot. Tim placed me in the car and walked over to the emergency entrance, where they were waiting to test him. I sat in the parking lot alone, wondering what had just happened. My life is no longer my own. My life has changed forever.

April 18, 1994   The hours of waiting turned into days of hellish pain and fear. The news the doctor gave me a few short days ago shocked my very soul beyond anything I have ever known.

April 25, 1994   Again I was seated in the same leather-covered chair as the same doctor told me that my husband had tested positive as well. Tim had stayed home this time, unable to face what he knew would be the truth. He had stayed in bed with his back to me, not wanting me to see the redness of his tear-soaked eyes. I cannot begin to explain the devastation I feel. I am not ready to face this. This can't be happening. Who or what has taken my life from me? It was only supposed to be a simple hysterectomy and reconstructive surgery, not HIV. Death is so paramount, so final. I know I'm about to die.

10:30 the same morning   I drove around the streets for over an hour, unaware of where I was. Nothing looked the same anymore. Somehow, streets, avenues, intersections and even stop signs had changed. I was filled with rage because I had to deliver the news to Tim that he had also tested positive. The small thread of hope that he would not test positive had been ripped away from me. I felt alone and completely isolated. I was terrified, I trembled with fear. I was in pain from the surgery. Would you cry if this were happening to you?

Separately, Tim and I withdrew to deal with this unwelcome news. He was feeling angry, frustrated, enraged and having a very difficult time not drinking after receiving this news. Years of fighting, unsuccessfully, the disease of alcoholism, treatment centers, denial and now this. So many feelings yet to be discussed, including suicide, which we both have considered but not spoken of. We are both hit with this news, and thinking rationally is not an option at this point. I am so very afraid for myself and Tim. Our dreams and plans for life have been taken away by HIV/AIDS. I have no idea what HIV is, let alone what it will do to us.

We have listened to news reports in the past and seen movies about HIV/AIDS, but we never considered that it would enter into the Morley household. It was always outside, in someone else's family. Gay people, high-risk people, hemophiliacs, drug users get this, not us. Not a couple married for over ten years. Not us, not me! This news eats at me. What will I do to stay sane?

May 6, 1994   I have begun to read anything I can get my hands on, but it's difficult to find information about women and HIV, so

I read articles that pertain to men and HIV/AIDS. I have to educate myself. Like most Americans, I know only what the media have put on that little square box that sits center stage in our homes and in the newspaper articles that are written by opinionated reporters. As of today, I have started researching and learning about the virus that now lives within us, within *me*. Where did it come from? How did it happen? Why me? Why both of us? Will we both die and leave the children to be raised by my mother, or someone?

May 7, 1994   Together, Tim and I begin work on planning our deaths. Living wills, wills and requests for property distribution have occupied our minds for the past few weeks. It has become the business at hand. I feel compelled to pack as much living into today as possible. Everything on television these days is related to sexually transmitted diseases, STDs. It won't go away. I feel surrounded, engulfed by HIV. God, please make it go away. I, we, deserve better than this. HIV/AIDS seems to be everywhere, even in our bed. The measure of my misery has appeared between us. The messenger of misery has come to pay a visit. Truly, life has changed. Will I ever get past it? I think not.

2:00 A.M. / unable to sleep   Finding the words to tell my children that Mom and Dad are HIV-positive will not happen any time soon. I can't tell myself yet. We have not told anyone in the family. We have no idea how our parents will take the news. We don't want to cause our family disgrace or have them reject us, and we don't want to field questions we have no answers to.

May 8, 1994   Today I know how the lepers, the social outcasts, felt in the midst of despair — searching for answers and finding none, looking to God and asking for His healing. This family, my family, is so very close, I can tell that the children know something seems different about me. "Babies, I am different." Oh, how I wish I could tell them, but I have no words to explain this living nightmare, this invasion of the enemy. Writing is the only way I find sanity.

May 10, 1994   Confusion. I have done little these days. Finding myself vegetating, looking but not seeing, listening but not hearing is not strange behavior for me. Feelings of drowning overwhelm me without warning. For moments at a time I am able to put it aside, but only for a moment. Finding reasons to get up in the morning has been difficult. Tim heard through one of his Narcotics Anonymous meetings about a place called Nashville Cares. Someone suggested that he and I go there for help in dealing with the thousands of questions and concerns we have.

May 12, 1994 / Nashville Cares I met Lisa today, the only other woman I know who is HIV-positive. Lisa has dark reddish blond hair that hangs to her shoulders. Her hands are small, her dress neat, her words filled with compassion. When we met this morning, she could tell that I was a mess and filled with questions about HIV/AIDS. She took me in her arms at once and told me, "You'll be OK, I'm here and you can talk to me." There was no way I believed her, but meeting someone else with HIV was indeed a great comfort to me. Spending time with her, listening to her tell me what she has been through, gave me a small sense of hope for the moment. I feel that my relationship with Lisa will become a very important one, and her courage will help sustain me. I am finding that HIV is bigger than me, it's bigger than anything I could have imagined.

It seems my plate is quite full. Like Lisa and so many others, I have lived with and through so much. I'm reminded of the saying, "God does not give us more than we can handle." With tear-filled eyes I do not welcome the challenge of HIV/AIDS. It is and always will be an intrusion in my life.

May 14, 1994 Burdened with worry, I think that I must have things taken care of before something happens to Tim or me. Changes in my body may be occurring, and I have no control over it. I've made arrangements for the children to spend the summer in Michigan with Grandma. My mother is always happy to have her only grandchildren come. I said nothing about HIV.

I am reminded of my childhood since speaking with her. Dreams of younger days fill my head at night. Thoughts of today and HIV fill my waking hours.

Midnight, again sleep won't come My mind keeps going back to younger days and years past. I lived in Catholic foster homes until the age of three, when my parents adopted me. I have some memories, but it all seems so long ago. My grandmother told me at age nine that I was adopted. Adoption was an issue better left undealt with in my family, and confusion about adoption remained throughout my childhood. My older brother Melvin was adopted too, but he was treated differently by our mother. Feeling rejection by both mothers — one I never will know and the other I so desperately wanted to know — left me to figure out life for myself.

I grew up in a house where I felt little love. My family was not the kind for hugs and kisses, not big on birthdays or "I love you's." Yet unspoken love was there. Spending most of my time in my bedroom by myself, with the things that were dear to me, I felt I had to be strong and independent. Mother would hold me and sing to me when I was very young, but the closeness soon changed. Things were so hard for her generation. I wonder if the distance I felt was her way of protecting me from the world.

My mother told me she loved me after I grew up. She did the best she could under the circumstances, I guess, but at the time, I felt removed from our relationship. Lessons about sex, boys, smoking, drugs and life in general were learned from friends — not a good teacher.

My father adored me when I was very young, but that changed as I grew older. My father was around but somehow always in the shadow of my mother. He worked every day for thirty years, never missing a day, except for the Detroit Tigers' opening day. He was not an easy man to talk to, so after learning that it was best to be seen rather than heard, I began to stay out of his way. My doll was my best friend, and in her I would confide my pain, tears and happiness. My father died two months after my son Brandon was born.

When I was adopted, the adoption agency told my mother that I should be put in dance classes because I loved music. I spent the next twenty-five years in dance. Learning and eventually teaching, I went to Hartford, Connecticut's Albano Ballet Academy and spent two years in dance/theater college. During my stay, I lived with gay and straight students. Dance and theater was my life for years, and the time I spent in college taught me much. It was my first experience living away from home. Among other things, I was taught that discrimination occurs not only due to color but also because of one's sexual preference.

By contrast, Tim was born third in a family of four children. With one brother being eight years older, his sister six years older, and his other brother eight years younger, there was little sibling bonding. Even though he felt alone at times, he says that he had a happy childhood. Though his heritage was Native American, it was not a part of his daily life.

When he was a teenager, his mother really didn't know what he was doing and could not keep track of him. He was always into something, but try as she did, she had no idea what he was up to. I believe that his parents had no idea he was into drinking and drugging at age thirteen. I suppose they did the best they could, because Tim's parents love him deeply and would not have condoned most of the things he did, had they known.

In all of this reflecting, I am left with this thought: A mother's love is a precious gift, one to hold close, one of unmeasurable fortitude. We look for love at home, in Mom, to hear her heartbeat against one's cheek as she gives what only a mother can. Such safeness and warmth are found in no other relationship. Mothers teach us how to love and show us that we are worth loving.

Dads are more than strong; they are the men who guide with firm, gentle hands and make all bad things end. They are the beginning of male relationships for girls who know nothing about life and the teachers of manhood to young-minded boys who search for wisdom in the male figures in their lives.

Things were great between Tim and me for a very long time. We did everything together. Our togetherness and closeness worked for us. Our relationship was strong, we were together because we wanted to be. Total unconditional love was finally mine — warm love in a relationship was ours. Then his drinking caught up with us and gradually took control of him. I could see how alcohol was destroying him yet could do nothing to stop it.

Alcohol almost destroyed our marriage and this family, but time and prayer have seen us through. Our history of unconditional love won the battle over alcoholism. But it was a difficult struggle. The two years of off-and-on separations and Tim's affair had us all wondering if we would ever be a family again. At the time, I thought that my life would never come correct. Tim needed us, and we needed him. Need was always a big word for me, and in order to be complete, we put our pride second and our marriage and family first.

This is what I would like to say to my children: Everyone makes mistakes as parents. Learn from them and move forward. Don't live life in regret, or "if only." Get up, get out and give it your all. Go after what you want and don't stop until you get it, then go after something else. Just don't stop. Growth takes a strong will and a patient heart.

May 19, 1994   No one in my life has given me what Tim has. We are meant to be like rain in the summer — warm, gentle love. Trips like our honeymoon in Hearst, Canada, will never be forgotten. Making a life for the children was and is our ultimate goal. Finding out how to do that while having HIV is the trick I don't have the skill or knowledge for. Sometimes I don't know what to think since becoming HIV-positive. At this point in time, I think it means eventual death. If I have taught my children anything in life, let it be Faith. Money, cars, houses or things will never give you what faith in Jesus Christ will give you, nor will they ever give you security. Throughout the years, my faith has been tested, but my God has always been there for me, even when I didn't think He was listening.

May 20, 1994   Act as if you have faith, and faith will be given to you. Example: There was a slight rain shortly after our diagnoses, and as I stood outside looking up, I asked the Lord to be with me throughout my life and at the end. At that moment, a loud thundering sound rang out, and I knew that He would be with me forever.

He has answered my prayer of salvation. Death is a part of life, and for anyone to deny the possibility of death is definitely not positive thinking. It takes energy to live in denial. A danger sign of denial is when we don't know it is happening to us; therefore, we are angry at those around us when topics come up that we are trying to avoid. Unconscious denial is often a friend to HIV/AIDS. Not facing the truth is much easier than facing

HIV/AIDS. Confronting the reality, and releasing one's negative energy surrounding HIV, allows one to focus on the now and the positiveness of today. Finding positiveness in a pandemic illness of this magnitude takes more than most of us are willing to give.

My values today are completely different from a year ago. I thought I had a life before April 12. I'm in a state of confusion. Today I am reading Arthur Ashe's book, and it encourages me to think about what I want to do with the rest of my time on earth. His views on life encourage me to continue to write. He also casts small glances of light in what has now become a dark life with little hope. HIV/AIDS has in fact changed my life, and now I must somehow get over the shock and begin dealing with it; that's the hard part.

Relinquishing myself to this is beyond me. It's in my head. It doesn't ever leave me for long. I feel overwhelmed at times. Keeping it from my children is not easy. It seems as though the everyday things of life are the hardest for me to deal with. Often I tell myself "Congress is in session" in my head; there's a debate going on, and I can't make a damn decision. Life has a way of moving on, and we have to move with it or be dragged through it. The sun will rise tomorrow whether we want it to or not. Getting with the program of HIV/AIDS is at hand. I call Lisa often. She helps every time I need her, with "I love you, Catherine," and "You are not alone." It seems she cradles me with her words of experience. I am trying to learn everything I can from her. I've been clinging to her since that first hug.

May 23, 1994 Keeping this journal has become important to me. Tim and Lisa encourage me to continue to write. When I write, I am in control, not HIV. Writing is the key to my sanity. If I could not write, I would have no voice.

July 5, 1994 / Changes I read everything I can get my hands on, now that I know that we are not about to drop dead. Thanks, Lisa. I need to know how to take care of myself and Tim. I have to learn to cook differently. I am learning about food and medications, as well as women with HIV and how it affects us differently from men. We continue to keep the horrific secret and the fear from the children.

Feelings of striking out come upon me often. Strike one, I am a woman; strike two, I am a black woman; strike three, I have HIV/-AIDS. Black women, again, are the minority within the minority. We suffer the most from this illness because we have less access to medications and treatments. I never understood how a black woman's worth always seems irrelevant. As with most things, we are the bottom of the bottom. No escape; there is no escape from its powerful grasp, it seems. Very little research is being done for us as blacks and as women. Most research is conducted for men. Why?

I want to fight for my life now. Outwardly, I appear the same, but every day when I look into the mirror, I see HIV growing inside me. Appearances are deceiving, and you can never know who is infected. Looking at myself hurts, because this body of God's has HIV/AIDS maturing within.

July 6, 1994   Stress, the stress of this is overwhelming me.

July 7, 1994   Tim is dealing with it differently. We talk about it when and only when I bring it up. Tim has found an escape. He can shelve this like he could his drinking. Denial, not dealing with it, is how he gets through. I wish I had the luxury of denial, but as with most things, I try to confront HIV/AIDS head-on. Knowing that he deals with things in his head alone makes me try to have conversations with him about his feelings. I need him to share his thoughts with me, in order for me to understand my own thoughts and not feel alone in them.

10:00 P.M., same day   What would people say if they knew? How would we be treated? How would you be treated? To date, only my best friend Fran, who has been like a sister to me since moving to Tennessee, and my wonderful friend LaVonna know. Both of them have sat with me, cooked, cleaned and taken care of the children when all I could see was bottom and emptiness. Questions of how people will react is baggage that we HIV-positive people carry. I've told them both about Lisa, the secretary at Nashville Cares, and how she has been a godsend.

Some of my feelings will never change, like the feelings of aloneness and separateness, somehow not a part of. Tim and I now plan
for the short term, not the long term. I can't think about family
vacations.

The foundation of this family starts here. Has the cornerstone
of this family collapsed?

July 8, 1994   Our family doctor since living in Tennessee, Dr.
Thomas Woolridge, recommended an HIV/AIDS clinic to Tim
and me. He is giving what he thinks is good advice, but I feel
rejected. I stood silent as his secretary made the appointment. I
trust Dr. Woolridge's advice. However, I don't like the idea of
going to an HIV/AIDS clinic. It seems different from spending time
with Lisa.

July 12, 1994 / First Clinic Visit   As I suspected, going to an
HIV/AIDS clinic for the first time was a bad memory. Long waits
in the waiting room were inevitable. Everyone there was being
seen for the same thing. Dr. Steven Raffanti, I am told, is an
HIV/AIDS and infectious disease specialist; therefore, the office is
very busy, and his practice is very demanding. Frequent emergen-
cies occurred, so I waited. It wasn't like a regular doctor's office
to me anyway. I knew as I looked around the room at the other
people sitting there that they too were HIV/AIDS infected or
affected. Some had small frames and could hardly walk, some
looked healthy, and some were very sick. I saw different stages of
myself in them. In the healthy ones I see myself as I was; in the sick
ones I saw myself as I know I will be. In the ones with the small
frames I saw myself as I might be.

Our family has been seeing the same doctor for over four years,
but I had to sit in some clinic that was totally unfamiliar to me.
Listening to others' conversations about the medications or the
drug trials they are on disturbed me deeply. I am no better or
worse than they, just in a different stage of HIV. Hundreds of questions raced through my head while waiting. I cried within so no
one would see.

After being seated in one of the rooms, I began to compose
myself. I asked what must have been thousands of questions, and

most were answered promptly in language I could understand. The nurse-practitioner, Beverly Maddox, was very compassionate and patient with me and took time to listen to my concerns and questions. Bev was assigned to work with us. Tim and I are planning the future of our health care. We're learning that so much can happen to an immune system that is compromised by HIV. We are faced with so many things that can and do go wrong.

My head is filled with new terms such as symptomatic, asymptomatic, viral loads, T8 ratio, T-cell counts above and below 500, opportunistic infections, lymph node swelling, night sweats — the list seems endless. Engulfed by symptom information, I was swamped by disease information: toxoplasmosis, *Mycobacterium avium* complex, mycobacterium tuberculosis, cryptococcosis, wasting syndrome, *Pneumocystic carinii* pneumonia, Kaposi's sarcoma, lymphomas, cytomegalovirus, candidiasis, and histoplasmosis, to name a few. Medications such as AZT, ddI, ddC, d4T, and Bactrim are only five that come to mind. Treatments or preventions for these and other illnesses are done to boost the immune system and to fight or control opportunistic infections. Believe me, there are many more medications, diseases and treatments I have yet to learn.

July 14, 1994   Tensions are high at home. The stress of HIV has caused friction between Tim and me. There are periods of isolation and detachment for us both. When we aren't totally inside ourselves we argue about nothing and everything. Keeping the changes that are occurring from one another leaves me cold. I don't dare mention the swollen lymph node in the back of my head or the pain it causes, because I don't want to worry him. In turn, Tim tries to keeps the stomach problems he is having from me. As his wife, my insight tells me his pain is worsening.

July 18, 1994 / Appointment with the Company's Medical Director
My doctors suggested that, before going back to work, I see the company's medical director. Talking with the director proved to be heartbreaking. I went to see him with letters from Dr. Madden, the surgeon; Bev, the nurse-practitioner at the clinic; Joan, a psychologist; and Rob, a counselor from Nashville Cares. The letters clearly explained my condition and their concerns about my

health. They asked for his help with job placement. I cannot go back to the job I was doing before the surgery because of the standing and the long ten-hour shifts. Also, because I've been gone so long, they have given the job to someone else. After reading the letters and listening to me confirm their content, his response was, "Go home, get your will made out, sell your house and set up someplace for your kids to live."

"What!" I said. I couldn't believe what I was hearing.

After all that "wonderful" advice, he told me, "There is nothing I can do to help you get placed on a nonproduction, nonrotating job, not even temporarily."

"But you are in charge of the medical department here, and I have restrictions that make it impossible for me to perform my usual job duties," I said. Concern for my work life was escalating at that point.

Tim and I had been successful in keeping the secret from the company, and I told the medical director that he was the only person who knew and that my doctors had suggested I go to him for help. His response was, "Don't worry. People will find out; you won't be able to keep this virus a secret. With all the sickness you got coming, you'll be lucky to have a job before it's over."

I begged him, please, not to show those letters to anyone else and not to keep them in my medical file. I even offered to take them back.

"No, I better hold on to them," he said. The director assured me that no one would see the letters and that he would keep them "under lock and key."

He offered no help, just unkind words. I couldn't believe what I was hearing. The man appeared cold and seemed to know less than I did. To make matters worse, this doctor was a black man — an insensitive, inexperienced black man who happened to be a doctor. I went to him, heart in hand, asking for his help in prolonging my work life, which is so very important to me and my family, and his reaction was so mean that I just couldn't understand. I was shaking, crying and totally hysterical by the time I left his office. Not wanting anyone to see me, I bolted out the door, ran to the car and drove home in a daze. I have great concern for my and Tim's future employment.

Later, Tim and I discussed the director's reactions. We can only hope that he keeps the letters locked away like he is supposed to. I do not understand why he would say that people will find out. Does that mean that he is going to tell others about us?

Bev, from the clinic, knew that I was going to see the company's medical director today, so she called, and I told her what he had said and his reaction to my request for job placement. She told me to just stay home and not worry about it. "Try to keep your stress level under control, Catherine. You've got to calm down." Easier said than done, especially when it's not your family's security on the line. I felt that the medical director had shown nothing but blatant discrimination, which was totally unexpected from a medical professional.

July 19, 1994   I'm back at work, but not really feeling well enough to be back. Bev wanted me to stay out longer, but I had to come back because my pay has been at 60 percent since June. The company has not changed since March; neither have its people. I was not put on a job, so I sat in the cafeteria waiting for a supervisor to find a job within my restrictions. This rotating schedule will be difficult to withstand.

July 20, 1994 / Tim's Visit to Comprehensive Care Clinic   He went for what was to be a regular checkup and was told that he needed to start taking Retrovir (AZT). After his appointment, we met in the Nashville Cares parking lot, where we stood holding each other and cried. I was shocked by the news and began to shake uncontrollably. I have read about AZT's strong toxic effects on the human body, and I began to panic. The reality of HIV has reared its ugly head more than ever. Oh my God, now what? I knew that Tim was sick and that something would be prescribed, but it doesn't make the news easier for either of us to take. Oh, my sweet babies. Oh! I didn't think to ask what his T-cell count is. I couldn't think of anything but AZT.

July 21, 1994   The children see books and articles about HIV/AIDS and are beginning to assume that something is wrong. They have not asked yet, but the tension is such that we must tell them soon. As Tim starts taking the medication, we have no idea what adverse reactions might be taking place within him. We both know that AZT causes damage to the liver as well as possible negative psychological reactions. Symptoms can fade within several weeks as taking AZT becomes part of your daily routine and the body becomes accustomed to it. However, I see danger on the road ahead and feel uncomfortable with the idea of this toxic drug being placed in a body that already has liver damage due to excessive drinking. All the studies I have read so far, which were conducted by medical specialists, bear out the utility or benefit of AZT in most HIV-infected people. Most every HIV/AIDS expert and doctor agrees that AZT is useful in treating HIV disease and that the benefits outweigh the risks for many people. Still, it does not bring me comfort knowing that my beloved husband must take this drug to survive this monster. His T-cell count is 500. I am not sure that the right decision was made.

In learning how to live with HIV, I have begun using meditation relaxation techniques, attending support groups and health benefits meetings and praying more. The need for a stronger relationship with God often comes with tragedy or life-changing conditions.

Praying is asking God's help; meditation is receiving His answer.

August 11, 1994 / WORTH My support group, WORTH, Women on Reasons to Heal, has without a doubt become my saving grace. Lisa and I formed WORTH because we were in need and knew that other women were out there feeling the same way. Lisa and I wrote letters to women who were on Nashville Cares' mailing list. Validation of a woman's needs and feelings is shared by each member. The support and understanding are wonderful. We have no agenda, no set rules or regulations, just the caring and giving of ourselves to one another. The bond I have with those women is slammin'. Talking, crying and laughing but, more importantly, sharing experiences and encouragement with one another is what we are about. Bringing one another up to date on the latest drug trials, medications and doctors' reports as well as nutrition, alternative treatments and ways of reaching other women who are alone is our purpose.

Moves

The eyes of many have been closed for a
    long time, they will see again.
The winds were silent, now howling rings.
    I give you me.
Caress me. Take me from the wilderness,
    bring me to HIV/AIDS.
There are no words that are found for the
    depth of my love for you.
Angels hear me clearly, listen.
A new beginning through once closed eyes
    and silent winds now moves.
Upheaval came, I was not prepared. Genteel
    hands lay upon HIV/AIDS.
Ride the winds on the wings of a raven
    searching for compassion.
Angels see me clearly, look.

My emotions run deep for the women of this group, because they give so much of themselves and care deeply for each member. The sisterhood is present each time one of us enters the hospital, because we are all WORTH. The relationship with other HIV/AIDS people is best described as one of constant learning. I find myself hanging on to words of wisdom, experience and hope. Words of hope — I could use more words of hope. Seems I forget how to hope, but then, after listening to those comforting words of life experience, hope does come. I find hope in the faces of people with HIV/AIDS. This group, for me, means give-and-take. Take only what you need and leave something behind.

August 12, 1994   Time has passed since Tim started AZT, and trouble with his arms has become burdensome for him. I saw him rubbing and stretching them in his sleep. He has mood swings that are caused by the medication or by drinking. Working in a manufacturing plant is in no way helping his condition. We have told no one at work about our health issues, which is definitely best for both of us. Experience with this large company has taught us to guard our privacy. Horror stories of losing jobs and insurance are discussed and are of great concern to almost every HIV/AIDS-infected or -affected family. The losses go far beyond material wealth. Not telling employers that you are HIV-positive in order to save your job is common practice. Association with this illness carries profound stigma.

The general public has missed the boat on the facts about HIV/AIDS due to early media coverage that was inadequate and persists in many parts of the country. Therefore, if you or someone you know is infected, you will sample the bitter taste of discrimination. The actions of the past continue to be a major problem in the epidemic. *Rich, poor, young, or old — we are all affected.*

State and federal legislation protects people against HIV/AIDS discrimination but does little about the harassment that occurs daily. Contemplating job loss when so much of my life is already in flux makes it necessary for Tim and me to choose taciturnity. We keep silent to protect ourselves and our families, like most infected people. Discrimination in the 1990s is very sophisticated, and finding ways to excuse someone from his or her job is easily done. Practicing tolerance of others' ignorance has become extremely hard these days.

August 15, 1994 I often wonder who knows. Then I tell myself that I am just being paranoid. Paranoid or not, I often wonder. Upon diagnosis, our names, we were told, had to be turned over to the state. I didn't understand that law, but we were told that we had to have our names turned in. What happens with that, no one could tell me. There is still so much I don't understand, nor can I get answers to questions, which leads to more confusion.

August 24, 1994 / Telling the Children The heat of the summer has come and gone, and the family has done a lot in the past few weeks — camping, boating, hang gliding, all in an attempt to bring more security and closeness to my precious family. Tim is doing better these days; we think the AZT is working for him. The time has come to tell Brandon and Aaron the truth about our medical status. I feel confident that they can handle it, but that does not alleviate the concern. They have seen Tim taking the medication but have been reluctant to ask what it is. Tim and I have had several conversations about what to say and how to say it so that they will understand. We don't want them to be alarmed or think that drastic changes are about to occur, so we choose our words carefully and go over anticipated questions. One thing we have decided is not to tell Jalyon now. Given her age (nine years old), we questioned her ability to understand. This is another time that HIV has made its presence known. We chose a Sunday, when Jalyon would be at a friend's house, to tell the boys. As the two of them sat on the floor in front of us, the prospect of the confusion and pain we were about to cause them brought me to tears. There was no single, simple way to tell them. We gave honest information at a level they could understand, rather than half-truths that we might regret later. I love them so much and wish we did not have this news to tell. We started by asking if they knew anything about HIV/AIDS.

"Only what they told us in school," they said.

Armed with books, pictures and pamphlets, we told them that their mother and father are HIV-positive. The shock of the news was spread across their beautiful faces. Scared and worried questions

came flooding out. "How did it happen? What will happen to you?
Do I have it?" Tears and hugs filled the room. Calmly and with great
care, we began answering their questions. I said, "At this point,
babies, we don't know how we became infected. We're still trying to
find out." Again I received my sons' hugs. "We found out shortly
after Mom's surgery. No, sons, you and your sister do not have HIV.
You have already been tested. We are both OK, but Dad has to take
medication to help his body fight the virus." More tears came.

With pictures, we showed them how the virus enters the body
and what it does to the cells of the body. The books and pictures
helped give visual aids of understanding. Having already talked
about drugs, sex, and alcohol made the conversation easier for
them, I hope. Thank God, we have always talked as a family about
making wise decisions regarding drugs and sex. They had no questions of blame or about which one of us had infected the other, only
concern for Mom and Dad. I had no sense of them pulling away or
having fear for themselves, only arms filled with love and hope. I
feel so blessed to have such a wonderful relationship with my children. Their loyalty and support are my comfort in this storm. As we
continue to talk about HIV/AIDS, the imprisonment of fear and isolation is finally over, and this family can now move forward without the secret that has captivated my husband and me. "Boys," I
heard myself say, "don't tell your friends. Remember what goes on
in this house stays in this house. We only want to protect you.
People can be so cruel. So for now, we must keep this quiet."
Rejection from their "friends" is what we are protecting them from.

My sons have no idea what the discrimination and rejection associated with HIV/AIDS could do to their accepting hearts. They are
so young and impressionable; this is happening to my beautiful children too. When this becomes public — and it will — the pain of
rejection will become another grieving process that I so want to
avoid. I will protect them with everything I have. My prayer now is
that my precious daughter will be given the same courage to understand and accept the news as well as her brothers have.

August 25, 1994 / Denial through Faith   The struggle within me
continues as I pick up the phone to call my mother. She is a very
religious woman. Faith for her is first, not second, nature. In the

past, she has spoken of her life and how faith has gotten her through cancer at the age of twenty-one, the death of her husband, and the deaths of her mother, sister and brother. I have called upon her faith several times in my life, and it has helped me through many difficult times. With that in mind, and after getting past all the small talk, I told her that Tim and I are HIV-positive. She was totally floored and wanted to know how this could happen to her only daughter. Her voice and reactions told me that she immediately went into total denial. She wanted to know how I got HIV/AIDS. Was it caused by the surgery I had? Did I have blood transfusions? She told me that I should not have had the surgery. I told her that it was too late, the surgery was over and had nothing to do with the facts.

My mother is strong, and as I cried and told her everything we had dealt with, her reaction was one of faith. " Catherine," she said, "Jesus loves you and Tim, and He will work this out. Somehow, God will work this out." After listening to me for about half an hour, telling all I knew about Tim's medication and its adverse reactions, she asked the basic questions regarding our health and whether we had told anyone else in the family or the children. Are they infected? My mother was using faith to deny my medical state, and I felt little support from her. Again the loneliness surrounds me and the feelings I am so accustomed to return. I need my mother, but she seems more worried that the family in Michigan might find out. She asked if I had told anyone. "No, Mother," I said, "I knew you wouldn't want anyone in the family to know." Appearances are very important to some people. Denying what goes on in one's family is a tremendously difficult task when you are faced with a life-threatening illness such as HIV/AIDS. I just want my mother to love me and accept me. By her not accepting my illness, I feel that she is not accepting me. These days, I come with the illness, and the two of us go hand and hand. She won't even say the words HIV/AIDS, so confronting it won't happen anytime soon. I don't have the strength to argue with her. She is unwilling to accept it at this point. She will have to take ownership sooner or later. HIV/AIDS is in her family to stay.

"Act natural. Pretend everything is the same." This was, in part, her advice to me. Pretend, how can I? Go back to "normal." What is that normal thing she mentioned? Hold your head up and go on with life was her advice. I hold my head up, to look for God. Again, HIV/AIDS has put a wedge between myself and an important relationship. My mind reels with thoughts I try to fight. I am an HIV-positive mother and *always* will be till the end.

Tim's call to his family was difficult as well. Tears filled his eyes before he began to speak. Composing himself, he said, "Mom, Catherine and I are HIV-positive, and we have been retested to make sure." His mother was shocked. He told her about his taking AZT and about his experience at the clinic. She wanted to know all about AZT and what effect it was having on him. I heard Tim trying to keep up with all her questions. Tears flowed freely on both sides of the phone line. His mother was so shaken that she had to give the phone to Tim's dad. Telling his parents made him face HIV all over again. A level of denial was taken away with that phone conversation. After spending about an hour talking about every aspect of the illness, he came to me drained and red faced. We cried and held each other as we lay in the warmth of our togetherness. It was a togetherness we hadn't shared in quite some time.

August 27, 1994   I asked the boys today if they had any more questions about our conversation. They both said no, but they keep asking, "Ma, are you and Dad all right?"

I watch to see if they are coping and wonder how well they really are handling the news. Telling them that we are fine doesn't seem to be enough, so I refer to points made during the two-hour conversation we had about HIV/AIDS.

August 28, 1994   WORTH, our women's group, was asked by the director of Comprehensive Care Clinic, the clinic we now go to for health care, to speak about the concerns of HIV-positive women who live in the Nashville area. The topics of discussion were the needs of working mothers who are sick, women as heads of households, dental care, gynecological issues and the aloneness we all share. We spoke of the simple things women need. Ryan White Act money is needed for women in Nashville.

I felt good leaving the meeting, but most importantly, I hope that WORTH can make a difference. Small rays of hope move in and out with the tides of life. My hope is that we will remain proactive in our community and continue to be called upon to speak about the needs of women who are HIV-positive and living with AIDS.

At the meeting there was a woman named Elsa, a member of WORTH, who had been told that day that she has full-blown AIDS. Elsa, a tall and very slim woman, had traveled in her weakened condition to many support groups. She spoke, in her raspy voice, about being twenty-one years old, married and unable to have children because she has become too weak. My heart sank. Life without my children, I can't imagine. Anyway, Elsa said that having AIDS was a "bitch." The women in the room, about twelve of us in all, listened carefully to how she has taken every medication the doctor has given her. Today it's thirty-eight pills, taken at different times, in a twenty-four-hour day. She carries a timer with her to help keep track.

Later the same evening   My birthday is in two days. I have listened to a young woman fifteen years younger than me tell me how short her life is. Elsa has nine T cells and three of those long-named diseases I told you about. She begins her morning by filling containers with different sizes, colors and shapes of medications that she will take throughout the day. At night, the alarm sounds, and she must wake up to take medication, which must remain at the same level in her body at all times. When she comes to group, she carries a telephone so that her husband can reach her to check on her, and in case of an emergency while she is driving. Frail and coughing, she does her best to educate the director of the clinic on how it is to live her life and the things she must do to survive one more day. She has to stop and catch her breath several times, and we all wait and give her time to speak. I told of the newness and devastation of living, learning and coping, of how important family and community are, as well the outreach and support we women deserve. The virus is in me, but it doesn't control my mouth or the mouths of any of the women present.

I look forward to my birthday very much.

August 29, 1994 / Chores   We, the family, went to the beach, and everyone had a wonderful time. It started rough, but after we organized the grill, food, sodas and swimwear, it was all forgotten. The kids swam and we all ate hot dogs. Brandon and Aaron talked about wanting a four-wheeler. They talked about it for almost an hour, telling Tim and me their reasons for ownership. We also talked about their chores being so messy. Then we had to hear, "but our grades are good." I finally told them to do some research on four-wheelers.

Tim and I realize that Aaron does do his chores and should not do without things because of the laziness of his brother and sister. It is not fair, but what should we do? Aaron has been known to be lazy too. True, not nearly as much as Brandon and Jalyon, but he has had his moments. Brandon wants things right now, but he is not willing to work for them. Life is going to surprise him, I think. Jalyon just wants to ride. I smiled at that one.

August 30, 1994 / My Birthday   Tim took the night off work and took me out to dinner at my favorite restaurant. His gifts to me were the perfume I like and a beautiful pair of earrings, but the gift I liked the most was his gift of himself. I cried a lot today — some happy tears, some sad. I thought a lot about Elsa today, trying to remember to thank God for myself. I am truly grateful to be thirty-six and have a husband and children who love me. Brandon came upstairs bright and early this morning with sleepy eyes to tell me that he loved me and to wish me happy birthday before leaving for school. Another happy thing was waking up and going downstairs and finding the den fixed up with birthday banners and balloons. Thanks, Jalyon. Also special was when Aaron gave me the birthday card he had made for me at school. This birthday means more than any other. I am happy to have lived to become thirty-six, but saddened by HIV also. I will not take another birthday for granted. Instead, I will rejoice in it and celebrate thankfully. Today I want all my children's love because it's my birthday. I love the three of them so much. Just saying it does not begin to express the true essence. I have a mother's love. They are my babies forever.

September 1, 1994 / Universal Terms Before/After Diagnosis   Joan, my psychologist, has become a trusted friend. I have been seeing her since the first week I was diagnosed. She was recommended by our family doctor. The first time I saw her, I felt an immediate connection. I wasn't sure how much she knew about HIV/AIDS, but that didn't matter to me. Not having experience with psychologists, I wanted there to be some kind of connection between us. I found our connection to be more important than what she knew about HIV/AIDS.

Together we learned, read and talked about HIV. She's clipped newspaper and magazine articles for me and told me about public radio talk shows and different HIV/AIDS clinics, doctors and facilities in Atlanta that she felt I should know about. She definitely keeps herself up to date on current HIV information. We talk about every aspect of my life, whether it pertains to HIV or not. In Joan I have found the freedom to talk about things I would never tell another living soul. Joan knows my heart. She has seen me through dealing with the doctor who did the original surgery. He was the one who ordered the HIV test without my knowledge. I heard that after learning that I was positive while I was on the operating table, he did not want to do the surgery or even touch me. But my gynecologist, Dr. Richard, whom I have been seeing for years, was there and prompted him to go on with it. After six months of not healing and my constant visits, the surgeon decided to cancel the balance I owed and told me that I may never fully recover. He encouraged me to continue my medical treatment with Dr. Richard. Joan was there through that miserable news. She's been my constant through this storm, the one person I could and still depend on to be there for me. No judgments, she listens and gets active in my life. She is a long-term participant. Joan's words of wisdom have been to "punt if you need to." I can't fix everything. I have learned that "downtime" in my life will come, but I try to recognize downtime for what it is. Downtime is when we take time out for ourselves. We all have bad days, bad weeks and even bad months, so we have to use downtime for the good it can bring — use it, learn from it, grow from it. Growth, along with most important things, takes time. She also encourages me to continue to write.

September 2, 1994   Last week the company's job placement department finally told me about a temporary assignment in another department in an adjoining building. I went there and was assigned to a particular area. The supervisor in that area began to come on to me immediately. He would call me away from my job, or he would wait until I was done and call me into a room away from everyone else, where he would make comments about my looks, my perfume, my hair, my health, my husband, his active sex life, the affairs he has had with other women at work and other comments about non-work-related issues. All this is very disturbing to me. I don't want him near me and have told him that. I hope that Tim and I don't run into him at the party tomorrow night.

September 3, 1994 / Company Party at the Ramada Inn   I really didn't want to go to this party, but several friends were going. Dancing was out of the question, so we sat and watched everyone. My supervisor from the plant cornered me outside the bathroom. He grabbed me. I pulled away. I have not told him about being HIV-positive, nor will I.

Tim and I didn't stay long after that. I am concerned about my job. How could he be so disrespectful to all of us? I feel bad about myself and I desperately want to tell Tim, but that would only cause more trouble. I don't know what to do.

September 5, 1994   The last few days have been OK. Yesterday we took everybody to Opryland. It was very tiring for me, but I think the kids had a good time. Opryland Theme Park was a birthday gift to Brandon and Aaron. I wanted so much to give them both more, but . . . .

Tim had a headache all day and was not in such a good mood. I think he tried to feel good, but it just wasn't happening. He's still bothered by stomach pains and bouts of diarrhea, losing weight and feeling tired all the time.

I am still hurting from the surgery, and it really gets on my nerves, so I don't talk about it much anymore. The pain still has me bent over, and the kids all tease me and say, "Mom, stand up straight." I have seen a total of five different doctors and have had more tests than I can count — believe me, I've tried. Tiring easily and having to rest often make me feel so old. My hands and feet are beginning to hurt, but I have been doing a good job keeping it from Tim and the children. Tim watches me closely, and I find myself watching him too. "Honey, you all right?" is said often. I'm worried about that supervisor. His behavior is sickening.

September 7, 1994 / Medical Understanding   Tim and I have reached an understanding about our health care. He will manage his, and I will manage mine. We will discuss our options and decisions with each other, but our individual health care choices will be personal choices. We agree that it will be best this way. Because my relationship with him is the single strongest force in my life, he will be the one most affected by my HIV status, and I by his. I believe that we can't be healthy if we are at war with each other. I am constantly reminding myself to find some form of positiveness in HIV/AIDS, because I know that anything else is self-defeating. We can become our own worst enemy and become self-destructive. Tim and I give what we can, as we can, when we can. Our lives together have been shared experiences, so we will share HIV/AIDS through loving hearts, standing by each other and believing in each other and our marriage, which has already suffered tremendously. Tim wants to know about the new medications but is not ready to participate in any drug trials. Me neither. He says that he is glad that other people are willing, but for him, the results of those trials are what he is after. He reads some of the information I get, and we discuss upcoming medications that are being experimented with.

He's become more open to discussion these days, and we talk freely about medications, friends and new treatments. But he doesn't talk about the feeling part. That has not yet entered our conversations, but I won't stop trying. Tim is a traditionalist and believes in Western medicine. I, on the other hand, want to know all the alternatives, including natural options, before making a decision. We are two independent people who respect each other's judgment but are not afraid to call the other on his or her stuff. I worry about him taking AZT, and if it were me, I truly don't know what I would do. I am glad I have not had to make that decision yet.

My feelings run deep about this virus, and I pray that one day I will have the words for all the feelings and emotions I hold. With both of us being HIV-positive, we have to set some kind of agenda for when we both are sick. Who will take care of whom? Who will take care of the children? Who will keep the house running, cook, grocery shop, pay bills, do laundry, help with homework, play taxi-cab driver, dole out punishments, attend teacher-parent conferences? It all takes work but can't be done when both parents are down with HIV and its many effects. We have to make our own personal decisions about the direction of our health care, but we will be there for each other and the children. We are determined to keep this family together, period.

September 9, 1994   I went to see Dr. Woolridge, our family doctor. He said that I have swollen lymph nodes in the back of my head and under my arms again. It hurts. He also said that I have infected sinuses and ears. I asked why I have so many infections, and he said that I just get them. He was in a hurry to leave, and I didn't have time to ask many questions. I don't see him as often as I used to, but he is a very good doctor and has continued to show interest in Tim and me. He knows our family medical history very well and has been our doctor since we first moved to Tennessee four years ago. He did not believe the test results when they were presented to him. At first, he thought that the test indicated herpes, so he ordered big horse-size pills for herpes. They turned out to be too big to take without tons of water. I would choke them down one at a time, having to take three. While I was on this medication, he ordered the second ELISA test, followed by the Western Blot test. These two tests are used to determine whether a person has the HIV antibody in her blood. I go out to his Nolensville office to keep him updated on the course of the illness. I trust him, and it is important for me to make sure that he knows what Bev at Comprehensive Care Clinic (Tim and I call it 3 Cs) is doing with our treatment. Dr. Woolridge has told me to come back and see him if I no longer agree with the course of treatment Bev gives. I told him about feeling abandoned when he sent us to the clinic, but reassuringly, he said, "Nonsense." I continue to take the children to see him, and we always talk about everyone in his family as well as ours.

12:00 A.M.   The virus itself is very small in size, literally microscopically small, but it is also the biggest thing man has ever known, bigger than some people, whether infected, affected or not affected yet, we are smaller than HIV/AIDS.

There are certain emotional responses to HIV infection. They are not fixed and do not come in any particular order, they just kind of happen. Some days I feel myself regressing back to when HIV and I first met. Today's mirror image seems deeper, or maybe I just look longer.

I am still so weak, and being on my feet for more than an hour tires me so. The kids still tell me to stand up. Tim's arms are hurting him. He has had three different cortisone shots so far, and Bev at 3 Cs told him he couldn't have any more because AZT and cortisone, which is a steroid, don't mix. He has been very supportive of the time I stayed home and says that working was easier for him knowing that I was home with the children. All the forgotten lunches and missed buses have shown me that the children need me.

During the time I was off, our lives took on a new change. Denying the children things they wanted hurt, but we did what we could. The word "no" was reluctantly accepted. I worry that I might lose my job because of the treatment I received from the medical director and because I still have not been placed on a team. If I had cancer or a heart attack, it would be difficult to tell the people at work, but once they learned of my situation, sympathy and kindness would be bestowed on me. They would even pass the basket for financial help. All kinds of collections were taken at work. The union representatives often came around collecting for this and that. But not one person has taken up a collection for families who are suffering from HIV/AIDS.

September 10, 1994 / Lost Dreams   Before our diagnoses, we were planning our dream vacation. Struggling, I thought that we had passed the garbage of separations, reconciliations, disappointments and Tim's drinking. I was looking to the future and the vacation of our lives, Australia. Tim has wanted to see Australia since he was young, and it was a great dream for me too. We were saving our money and had plans to have our passport pictures taken after I recuperated from surgery. We also wanted to see Europe and had talked about how it would be to travel to other countries together.

This dream has been one of the hardest things to let go of. Our financial difficulties since then have drained all the funds we had set aside. My recuperation has not been at all what we had hoped. The price of not working and being infected has touched us all. Brandon, Aaron and Jalyon were looking forward to staying with their grandma in Michigan and visiting all the aunts, uncles and cousins while Tim and I traveled the globe. I am so sorry our plans are ruined. The dream will remain only a dream.

September 11, 1994   Elsa came home with me yesterday from group because she wanted to "just hang out." We talked all day and half the night. I am glad we took the time to listen to each other. I learned a lot from her. She left the next day around three in the afternoon. Elsa and I shared our lives and laughed all night. She still has that awful cough and sometimes can't get her breath, but she stays on top of her medication with the help of her alarm. Jalyon hung out with us, and the three of us had a good time.

September 12, 1994 / Our Church   I went to see the priest at our church last Friday, and maybe he hasn't dealt with HIV/AIDS much, but he was not very helpful. He didn't have much to say and was visibly standoffish. I had had his counsel before, so I felt good going to see him. In the past, since attending St. Philip, I had spoken to him about our marital problems and Tim's drinking. Father Arnold had been very comforting and offered several ideas, including counseling Tim and me together. Apparently, HIV/AIDS was completely different. He told me that he felt sorry for me and that we should begin taking better care of ourselves, all of which is good advice, but it left me feeling empty and spiritually down. I sat listening with tears flowing. Trembling, I told him about my experience with the company doctor and my fears for our family's future. Father listened unmoved, offering nothing. I thanked him politely and went home. This was my touch with the Catholic Church. I had turned to the church, as many do, for spiritual uplift and a return to home. After talking to Tim about my conversation with the priest, we decided to look for a different church — one that encompasses everyone. It seems another change is coming.

September 14, 1994 / More Tests   I am scheduled for a CAT scan next week at Vanderbilt Medical Center. I've had so many tests since our diagnosis, and I am tired of the probing. I finally told Tim that I fainted yesterday, which was the second time this has happened. The first was at the grocery store, and after regaining myself, I hurried and picked myself up and acted like nothing had happened, looking around in embarrassment. The second time I began to realize that something was wrong. I have never fainted before and have no explanation for fainting now. Tim insisted that I tell the nurse practitioner so she could set up the CAT scan.

September 17, 1994 / Saturday Morning   Today was quiet for Jalyon and me. We stayed home and read. Brandon went to his friend Randy's house. Aaron and his dad went to play pool. Jalyon and I read a book about angels. She asked questions about angels and whether they are real. I told her, of course they are real; angels are another of God's gifts sent to comfort us. We also talked about miracles and what a miracle is. "With faith, Jalyon, miracles do happen." She wanted to know if she has angels of her own. I told her, "Yes. Look inside yourself and listen carefully. Your angel is near."

Report cards came out last Friday. I'm proud of them. Lord knows, I haven't been much help so far with their lessons. That must change.

Spending quiet time with my daughter was just what I needed. After everybody came home, we all watched movies and laughed.

September 18, 1994 / Sunday Afternoon   I talked to Elsa. She talked really strange about things she thought I should know about. When I told her that I had no idea what she was talking about, she became agitated and confused. She said, "Don't mind me; it's just the dementia." Dementia is an impairment of intellectual functioning. It has multiple symptoms and can range from mild to severe. Both long- and short-term memory can be impaired. Some people with advanced AIDS suffer from dementia, and some don't. Elsa has advanced AIDS.

There is $70 in the four-wheeler collection.

Tim is gone to his Narcotics Anonymous home group meeting, which he also attends every Wednesday he is off work. I guess being HIV-positive has made him look at his recovery more closely. He knows the twelve-step program word for word, but applying it is something quite different. He has told me that if everyone could apply the twelve-step philosophy to their lives, tolerance of others' differences would be more accepted. He has gotten himself a sponsor after talking about it for weeks. I think he is trying to stay sober since HIV and AZT have become a part of his life. Tim said, "I have spent the better part of my adult life struggling with the disease of alcoholism, and now I have another disease, HIV." He is going to meetings regularly.

October 6, 1994   I went out on sick leave yesterday. I am not feeling well. That supervisor from work called me at home this evening. I told him never to call my home again.

October 22, 1994   Things have been so difficult I have been unable to write.

November 8, 1994   My father has been dead thirteen years today. I often wonder how our lives would have been if he had lived. He would have loved his grandchildren and spent lots of time with them. I regret his passing and not knowing my children. His two grandsons would have been very special to him, and his only granddaughter would have been his world. He loved little girls.

My relationship with my father was definitely interesting. After I grew up, he came to respect me, but the closeness I was looking for was not there. I knew that he was proud of me, not because he said so, but because of the way his face would light up when I came around.

Jalyon got her school pictures today.

November 9, 1994   Last night was the best night Tim and I have spent together in a long time. Tim worked hard to make the evening very romantic and wonderful. He had a shrimp plate, apple cider, the hot tub, and great jazz music. We spent the evening in the hot tub. It was great to talk and spend time together. We both were able to put HIV away and not talk about it. He even had rose petals on the bed. I felt so wonderful and secure. Our marriage has suffered greatly because of HIV. Retreating from one another has changed the closeness we once had. Our sex life was one of passion. Like most married people, we enjoyed each other completely. HIV changed that. We have to use protection now. We have to put a barrier between us. Because we are both infected and the virus is different in each of us, we must take precautions not to reinfect the other. Yes, on top of everything else, we can reinfect each other if protection is not used each time sex happens. Even if only one partner is infected, protection must be used. Intimacy between us has become rare, and the less we have the farther apart we feel. So last night was really special.

November 10, 1994 / Conference　I have decided to go to the Women and HIV and AIDS Conference that is being held in Washington, D.C., next February. I would like to be a part of the solution working toward the goal, a cure for this virus. I am filled with warmth and comfort now because I have made this wonderful decision. Tim is happy for me and encourages me to go. He told me that he sees the fire in my eyes when I speak of the conference.

I want to share my story with those it may help and to help anyone who does not know that HIV/AIDS can and will kill. For the first time since being diagnosed, I can find some form of reason within.

I went back to work. The shift rotation at the plant goes like this: a week of ten-hour days, a week of ten-hour nights, a week of ten-hour split shifts and a week off.

November 11, 1994 / A Prayer Request　I am consumed with feelings of humbleness, feelings of being blessed — an inner peace. I have grown spiritually over the past few months and have grown in my faith and beliefs. It's a wonderful feeling and one I try desperately to hold on to. It slips away and I get lost at times, but I am working on the reconstruction of my faith. Trying to keep this feeling within is sometimes not easy. I try to keep God close — surrounding me, surrounding my faith. I would like to give my life to God. I'd like to work in the fight against HIV and AIDS. I want God's words to come from my mouth as I speak against the lack of education that has

Wedding day. Catherine with her mother and Tim.

occurred among our youth or for universal health care for every American. We need to be educated. I believe that people should know about HIV infection and how it will affect their lives.

I have to believe that there is a divine reason that I have lived the life I have and have been chosen to be exposed to this illness. My life has been a course filled with so many ups and downs. Now, on the other side of it all, I find more faith. I pray that the Lord keeps His hands on my children every moment of their lives. Please pray for everyone in need of love and prayer.

November 13, 1994   I just got off the phone with Mother. We discussed my decision to go to Washington, D.C., and about my speaking publicly. She is still concerned that I may begin telling members of the family about our secret. I think that she is concerned about their reaction to us. How will it affect them, I wonder? Seems like only the rich or well known can go public with this illness. People like me, who live an average life and are unknown, are the ones who have to hide it from everyone to make sure that our families don't suffer. I care about how my efforts to do something will affect my husband and children.

Lisa asked me to speak at a high school in Nashville about HIV/AIDS. They want me to speak from the point of view of a mother with young teenagers. It will take time for my mother to get used to other people knowing. After all, she and the relatives live in Michigan. I want to help, but not at the expense of my immediate family. The urge to speak publicly about HIV and mothering grows within me. Yet I'm filled with questions about what to do. If I try to help others by educating them so that they won't get this disease, will I hurt my own family?

November 30, 1994 I picked Jalyon up from school early for her dentist's appointment. She needs five teeth pulled. While running around town, a feeling of total fatigue — too tired to move — came.

December 1, 1994 / A Moment Locked in My Heart Yesterday Jalyon found Ace the cat dead in the middle of the street when she came home from school. Aaron and Brandon buried him on the hill behind the house. I will never forget the three of them standing on the hill beside his grave that Aaron had made a cross for. I will hold that picture in my heart as long as I live. Brandon stood on the tree that had fallen from the recent ice storm, Aaron sat on the ground next to the fallen tree, one leg bent and the other straight. Jalyon was standing next to the grave with her finger in her mouth, her big bright eyes filling with tears as she looked down at me. I stood at the bottom of the hill filled with so much love for all of them. Kids, this has been a very hard year for me, but I hold on to the small gifts in life and keep them near me. As I saw the grief in their faces over the death of the family cat, I could not help imagining what they might feel if it was Tim's or my grave they were standing around.

December 7, 1994 / Sickness and Death The family is driving to Michigan in the morning. I don't look forward to attending Arcella's funeral. She was my favorite aunt.

Tim and I looked at each other, without words, when we got the news of her death. But we both were thinking, it could be us. This has to be hard on my mother. I worry about her getting through

In Training

Wandering through life I have often asked "why?"
  without getting an answer.
Today I don't ask, I just wonder.
HIV/AIDS has changed everything for me.
Growth is at hand. Struggling to find reason has
  currently become of the utmost importance.
Yesterdays are filled with whys.
Tomorrows are filled with healing and grace.
Look to the soul of your self for deeper
  understanding.
Journey inward through your heart, past the mind,
  beyond the body into the core of you and there
  will be the answer.
Cleaning the core of one's soul takes mastery,
  perfection and reflection.
God will be along.
His gifts will sustain me, give me comfort, and
  ease the pain.
Learn yourself first.
Trust you, and the ability to know your dreams will
  be near you.
Our lives are cut with the knife of illness, suffering
  and anger.
Let go.
Where do you go when you don't have the
  answer?

this. She and her sister were very close and saw each other most every day. They had traveled together and talked on the phone daily, and for the past six months, Mother had taken Arcella to the hospital for her chemotherapy treatments. Mother never gave up hope when the doctors told the family that they had found cancer. She never stopped praying and never stopped believing.

December 13, 1994 / Back from up North We stayed just long enough for the funeral services. When we got to Mom's house, I had to lie down because I was drained from the ride. I came in, said the hellos, gave out hugs, and went straight to the couch. There I stayed. I couldn't move, I didn't eat. My mother covered me and stayed with me until she went to bed. She talked again about the importance of not telling any family members. I again agreed, but this time it was for her sake, not mine. She said that she wants to come to Tennessee for Christmas. The next morning, everyone was busy getting ready to attend the services, but I was finding it difficult to get up. This feeling of total fatigue is unlike anything I have ever felt. It goes beyond tired. It becomes a big deal just to lift my arm. When we got home, I found that Bev had left a message on the answering machine, saying that she had called in a prescription for the numbness I am now having in my hands and feet.

December 16, 1994 Jalyon got those five teeth pulled today. She was so good and I was so proud of her. She came home and laid down for a short time but soon bounced back and was ready to eat dinner by evening.

December 23, 1994 Mom's here, and it's great having her. We all went shopping and rode around looking at Christmas lights. The hills of Brentwood were spectacular and breathtaking, as was the skyline of Nashville. She loves looking at all the richness of the hills that surround us. I have never enjoyed my mother more than I have this time. We shared thoughts that had gone unspoken and bridged some of the gap between us. I am content with my relationship with my mother. I will lock this time spent with her in my heart forever, just like the scene of the kids on the hill in the backyard.

December 27, 1994   My mother's leaving tomorrow.

Note to my children   Put people around you that will help and encourage you. Choose a friend wisely. Negative comments from people who are special to you can be worse than the good you try to accomplish. Negative things will happen to you regardless of what or who you are. You are wonderful people, and you have God-given talent. I want to encourage you and tell you that you can accomplish anything. Follow your dreams and your heart. Sometimes it's best to be an active listener rather than a participant. Remember to watch, and learn first, before jumping into things that may have the potential to hurt you. Relationships change, sometimes better, sometimes not. ■

1995

Blessed is the man that walkest not in the council of
the ungodly, nor standeth in the way of sinners,
nor sitteth in the seat of the scornful.
But his delight is in the law of the Lord; and in his
law does he meditate night and day.
And he shall be like a tree planted by the rivers of
water, that bringeth forth his fruit in his season;
his leaf also shall not wither; and whatsoever he
doeth shall prosper.
The ungodly are not so: but are driven like the
chaff which the wind driveth away.
Therefore the ungodly shall not stand in the
judgment, nor sinners in the congregation of the
righteous.
For the Lord knoweth the way of the righteous: but
the way of the ungodly shall perish.

Psalm 1, King James Version

Hear me when I call, O God of my righteousness:
thou hast enlarged me when I was in distress;
have mercy upon me, and hear my prayer.
O ye sons of men, how long will ye turn my glory
into shame? How long will ye love vanity and seek
after leasing?   Selah.
But know that the Lord hath set apart him that is
godly for himself: the Lord will hear when I call
unto him.

Stand in awe and sin not: commune with your own
heart upon your bed, and be still.   Selah.
Offer the sacrifices of righteousness, and put your
trust in the Lord.
There be many that say, Who will show us any
good? Lord, lift thou up the light of thy
countenance upon us.
Thou hast put gladness in my heart, more than in
the time that their corn and their wine increased.
I will both lay me down in peace, and sleep: for
thou, Lord, only makest me dwell in safety.

Psalm 4, King James Version

Kings' daughters were among thy honourable
women: upon thy right hand did stand the queen
in gold of Ophir.
Hearken, O daughter, and consider, and incline
thine ear; forget also thine own people, and thy
father's house.
So shall the king greatly desire thy beauty: for he is
thy Lord; and worship thou him.
And the daughter of Tyre shall be there with a gift;
even the rich among the people shall intreat thy
favour.
The king's daughter is all glorious within: her
clothing is of wrought gold.
She shall be brought unto the king in raiment of
needlework: the virgins her companions that
follow her shall be brought unto thee.
With gladness and rejoicing shall they be brought:
they shall enter into the king's palace.
Instead of thy fathers shall be thy children, whom
thou mayest make princes in all the earth.
I will make thy name to be remembered in all
generations: therefore shall the people praise thee
for ever and ever.

Psalm 45:9–17, King James Version

January 5, 1995 / Parenting   Once you become a parent, you are a parent forever. Leaving, or not sharing in your child's life, won't change that fact. That's why young people should take their time before becoming parents. Live life, explore life, enjoy life, have memories before having babies. Have great loving relationships. It is very difficult to have a relationship with your child when you have become a part-time, sometime, convenient-time, half-time, no-time parent. Giving your child your values and your experience can't happen if you are not around. Anyone can make a baby, it's who raises and cares for the child that matters.

January 12, 1995   Went to an HIV/AIDS conference in Fort Campbell, Kentucky, with my good friend Deidre, from WORTH, and a guy named Joe to hear speakers and get updated information. It was very informative. I watched and listened to medical personnel speak about patients' treatments, clinical trials and new medications.

Deidre spoke about how she became infected: a young college student, first time away from home and having unsafe sex with a young man she had been dating for a few months. She reflected, with tear-filled eyes, on the decision she had made. She remembered asking him if he had any sexually transmitted diseases. He laughed and said no, so she had unprotected sex with him. Young and inexperienced, Deidre was drawn to this good-looking, clean-cut, muscle-bound college man. One lesson here is that asking someone if they have any STDs and having unsafe sex is *not* wise. Deidre learned the hard way that asking does not mean that the person will be honest, and sex, safe or not, is not worth your life.

Today Deidre has full-blown AIDS, is twenty-five years old and has chosen not to have children. She has been married for five years to a man who does not have the virus. Deidre found out she had AIDS six weeks before she was to marry her husband. She can never have unprotected sex with her husband; therefore, they will never have children.

Joe, a twenty-nine-year-old man, spoke about how he abused drugs for most of his teenage years and became infected. He too had unprotected sex with many women and didn't think that "it" could happen to him. He thought that "it" happened only to gays and blacks. He really didn't think "it" would affect him. Living in Texas and the youngest of five children, Joe was twelve when his father died of cancer. Young, wild and full of drugs, Joe held the anger within. One of his friends was sick, so he went to a clinic with him. While there, he decided to be tested. His friend had a cold and was given antibiotics; Joe was told that he had AIDS. His world collapsed around him, he recalled. He became enraged and continued to use drugs more than ever. Emotionally and physically, Joe got sicker until he was no longer able to go out and get drugs. He decided to move to Tennessee and get away from his drug-abusing friends in order to make some sense of his life. Today Joe's CD4 (T-cell) count is nine; he is on disability, living alone in a room provided by Nashville Cares and dependent on Meals-on-Wheels to bring food. He is still angry and an emotional wreck, but he's trying to find a job to give him some sense of himself.

Relationships in and of themselves are complicated enough, but when sex enters into a relationship, hormones take over, intelligence seems to drain out and the passion of the moment rules. Drugs only serve to complicate things. Think about the risks of STDs, pregnancy and death. Not having sex is a choice. Having unprotected sex is a choice. Whichever you choose, please think.

January 16, 1995 / Martin Luther King Jr. Day MLK day and the kids are out of school. Aaron's best friend, Cassidy, came over and they seemed to have a good time. Tim had been drinking last night and fell asleep on the couch. Aaron and his friend found three large empty Budweiser bottles hidden under a tire in the garage. I felt angry that Tim's old behavior was continuing and embarrassed at the boys finding the bottles.

Jalyon and I went to see my best friend Fran today. She told me how much her family enjoyed the cake I baked them for Christmas. I also spoke with Deidre, who has been sick for days. She talked about the fatigue and nausea she feels and the reactions she is having to the different medications she's taking. She had been on AZT for a long time, but the doctors took her off it because her body became immune to it and it was no longer helping her. They are trying her on other medications, so she waits to see what her reaction will be. I pray for all those who are affected and infected by HIV/AIDS. My heart is heavy for all of us.

January 19, 1995 / Reading the Psalms At times I wonder: has someone changed lives with me when I wasn't looking? Life has become an HIV/AIDS soap opera, worse than *General Hospital*. The only problem is, this is real and I can't turn it off or change channels. Keeping the faith can be difficult at times. It doesn't mean I don't believe or that my faith is diminishing; it simply means that faith is hard when I'm in the throes of life and have dirt all over myself. Bathing doesn't seem to get me clean enough.

We have to play with the hand we're dealt. Before life takes its toll and things get out of hand, I read Psalms. I look to the Lord for wisdom no man can give. He knows my heart and soul. Always walk with God.

January 20, 1995 The supervisor from the plant continues to call my home. When I'm not at work due to illness, taking a vacation or whatever reason, he calls. His continued advances toward me have become unbearable. Tim and I talked about the situation. Tim was angry. I cautioned him.

January 27, 1995 I have that constant headache I seem to keep getting. Glandular swelling continues. I haven't written in a while. I am feeling pretty low these days and have not had the energy to write. Seems the support system I have carefully constructed for my well-being is not working lately. I have a lot on my mind and don't want to share those thoughts. Congress is in session in my head and can't make a damn decision. I know I will get past this and will begin to pick myself up again soon, because it is my nature to continue to fight.

February 2, 1995   Tim talked to me tonight. He spoke of the anger he has — anger about being HIV-positive and anger about spending his life wrapped in a body that is addicted to alcohol. He spoke of dying. He does not want AIDS to disable him in the ways he has seen and read about. He has spent a lot of time thinking about how better off we would be if he died when his time came, instead of a slow, lingering death. He feels selfish and is angry about feeling selfish. I think that he is angry about feeling guilty, and guilty about feeling angry. He said that he had not been drinking when I asked, nor had he been crying, but the emotional pain he struggles with daily does cause him to drink, and the anger surrounding his surrendering to alcohol explodes in his head. He told me, "It is no excuse for drinking, but I do wonder why, at this point, I need an excuse." I told him it was because he has a family that loves and needs him. He said that the illness people get with AIDS is enough to scare him and he won't go through that. I listened to him talk, and the anger filled the room. He laid down in front of the fire and slept. I tried to comfort him until he was asleep.

It has taken him all this time to come to grips with his illness, and he needs time to grieve. I am filled with so many emotions, words cannot say. I love my husband with all my heart, but I have no control over his actions. I wish he could take responsibility for this. I wish he could say he's sorry. I believe that if he hadn't had the affair and been drinking, we would not be HIV-positive. Our healing can't begin without facing the truth.

February 9, 1995 / A Dream or Nightmare   The kids have been out of school for the past two days due to the snow. Everything shuts down in Tennessee when it snows, and the children love sledding down the hills that surround our house. They have told me it's like being in Michigan without the weather being so cold.

I had a dream that disturbed me and kept me up afterward. There was a happy little girl about seven or eight years old on a playground swing. Seems to me the dream was taking place in the 1960s because of the way she was dressed and the cars and buildings I saw. Anyway, she swung alone but didn't mind being alone. I could sense her contentment within herself because she had a happy spirit. I could relate to her so well. She was dressed in a bright-colored print dress with bows in her hair and black patent leather shoes with white socks turned down at the ankles. She swung and sang as a car full of young boys came slowly down the street behind her. The windows were down, and I saw the gun with a long barrel and silencer. In slow motion, he raised and pointed the gun out the open window. As they drove by, one of them from the backseat shot her. She could not understand why, but as she realized the pain, she fell off the swing and crawled to a corner of the playground, in silence and with no tears, where an old tire was laying and curled up. She was shot in the back, and pain and confusion raced through her. Her pretty print dress was bloodstained, and the socks she wore were now dirty. As I dreamed I felt her slipping away and becoming still. I felt myself becoming her, feeling the shock, filled with questions of why. This dream disturbed me deeply. What do you think it was about?

February 10, 1995   There have been so many dark days, so many uncertain days, so many days of pain, questions with no answers, prayers seemingly unanswered.

Remember, God's gift to us is life; what we do with our lives is our gift to God. Be open to differences, differences in people, in thinking and ideas. Choose your own way, make your own path where there is no path and leave a trail. Great people in history had setbacks, but the difference in them and others is recognizing a setback as temporary. Things will get better, they can't stay bad. Faith.

February 14, 1995   Making plans to attend the HIV Infection in Women conference in Washington, D.C., has kept me very busy. Deidre and I have been planning for months to go together, and I have been working on obtaining a scholarship from the sponsors. Deidre will get her scholarship through her job at Nashville Cares. I, however, had to apply through the conference sponsors in order to help defray the $825 it will take to get me to Washington. I did not get the conference scholarship.

I met a wonderful woman who has written a book about her brother, John Ford, who died of AIDS. Susan Ford Wiltshire is a kind, gentle spirit. She is a professor at Vanderbilt. She has dedicated her life to educating others on HIV/AIDS. Susan and I spoke over the phone, and I told her about my plans to attend the conference and how I needed help getting there, since I had been turned down by the conference scholarship committee. I told her that I could get most of the money from Metropolitan Interdenominational Church, and she offered to sponsor the rest.

Thanks, Aaron, for the hand-carved wooden box you made me for Valentine's Day. It is truly the greatest gift I could get. It is obviously from your heart. You worked long and hard on it. I will keep your gift long after this day has passed, and it will be on display for all who enter our home.

Tim took the children to a hockey game. I stayed home and wrote.

February 15, 1995   My hands are hurting very badly these days and have been since November. The burning and numbness bother me most. The pain is constant and wakes me most nights. Pain moves up my wrists and arms. My fingers lock and I lose control of my hands. Activities that this pain affects are driving and shifting gears, combing Jalyon's hair, opening jars and doors, holding pots and pans, yard work, writing, holding objects and everyday living. I have spent time thinking about what HIV is doing to me. I feel as if I am losing control over parts of my body due to HIV wreaking havoc.

February 17, 1995   I received a precious gift today. Susan Ford Wiltshire gave me her book titled *Seasons of Grief and Grace: A Sister's Story of AIDS*. I can't tell you how I felt when she handed me the book about her brother John Ford and her family's struggles facing AIDS and homosexuality. She writes from her soul. She is a wonderful woman, very compassionate and warm. I began reading it today and I'm taking it to Washington, D.C. Her book will be placed on display in our family bookcase.

February 26, 1995 / Conference Summary   I am so very grateful for the experience of attending this conference. Talking with and listening to women whose lives have been changed has validated my own life. It was a opportunity to connect with other women of all races and creeds, held together by the commonness of

HIV/AIDS. The air was charged with emotions. Women in all stages of HIV or AIDS gave of themselves with openness. Tears, anger, determination and sisterhood lit the room.

As I listened to speaker after speaker, I concluded that research has been done in every area under the sun. But still no cure. They have researched in and on every aspect of this illness. But still no cure. Speakers talked about drug usage, multipartnered women, unemployed and employed women, children as they relate to women, homeless women, all races of women, self-esteem in women, medication in women, ACTG 076, bisexual women, herbs, long-term survivors, social classes, uneducated and educated women, biological recurrences, and the list went on and on. But I did not hear anything that told me a cure is at hand. Studies about everything, but no cure. The workshops were packed with graphs, percentages, case studies and options, but no cure was presented.

AIDS among black women is up 28 percent. Women are the fastest growing population contracting HIV/AIDS. Women's treatment has been shelved since the onset. Women are dying faster than men, because research is so far behind with regard to women's issues. This explains why I had difficulty finding information about women and HIV/AIDS at the beginning.

Fourteen hundred women wanted answers that we did not get — answers from government officials who are not infected with HIV/AIDS. We were told by medical staff — mostly women — that results are forthcoming on studies that they personally have been part of. So many government hands working diligently with women's issues, but no cure on anyone's list. How will we ever get the government to understand until it walks in our shoes?

The history of women and HIV/AIDS dates back to the beginning of the pandemic. No cure. The epidemic is growing fast among young, uneducated, heterosexual women who are willing to please their partners in every way possible. Women take for granted that once married they do not have to worry about any STDs, let alone HIV/AIDS, so no condoms are used. Pleasing people is what we are taught from early childhood. We are dying in large numbers as we please the people we love.

Ignorance is not bliss; it can be deadly. When will the struggle end? My heart is heavy after listening to the town meeting portion of this seminar. The highly respected and well known CDC, Centers for Disease Control and Prevention, was disfavored by these women. My heart is so worn out as I listen to story after story about how the CDC has not moved forward fast enough.

The Act   The Ryan White Act's money, which is allocated by the government for HIV/AIDS research and benefits for all persons infected, is closely monitored by us as well. We want to know how and where this money is spent. The act itself is failing. Again, too many hands in the same pot, and not enough involvement of the people for whom the act was made.

Currently, the Ryan White Act does not cover those women who are in prisons. These women are getting out with HIV/AIDS and no treatment, education or knowledge. They are dying in prisons because they have the illness and are not being treated while incarcerated. The only help for these women is women — the ones who go into prisons to educate and give updated news to the inmates and corrections officers. HIV/AIDS-positive women in New York are going into the prisons to work on the issues of living with HIV/AIDS. How much clearer do we need to be? How many women, children, men and families will suffer before "they" listen?

Meanwhile, as the conference continues, Congress is looking into laws that would make every woman in the United States get tested for HIV when getting a pregnancy test. Where is the constitutionality in that? The law sounds good at first, but it could lead to women not obtaining prenatal care. This is the ACTG 076 project I spoke of earlier. Are there any laws in the works for all men to be tested? Why does our health care insurance not cover all treatments that will keep us alive or prolong life? Why in 1995 do we not have health care for all?

Greg Louganis goes public as the conference continues.

Late the same evening — reflections   As I prepare to leave Washington, D.C., my thoughts drift back to the faces of those women. I can still hear truths and advocacy for universal health care. Common issues around stigma, spirituality, women's health care, when to start medications, should AZT be taken and daily living have been my concern, and that concern was shared by the women I spent countless hours talking with. We must create public awareness about what the illness does both inwardly and outwardly — stressing unity!

Indeed, I am overwhelmed by the prospect of what my future will be. I am, however, dedicating what and who I am to the fight. I get my direction from God and move forward. My prayer is for strength, the love of my family, and support of my most dear friends. I thank my children for giving me this time to learn and grow at this conference. We all have much work ahead!

February 28, 1995   My dear friend Deidre told me today that she is concerned about me. She wanted to know if I am ready to go public with my HIV status. She gives me lots to think about; she has that effect on me. Deidre knows firsthand about public reactions, because her job at Nashville Cares is the First-Person Program coordinator. She travels to schools, churches and businesses, educating people about HIV/AIDS. I have traveled with her several times and have experienced the reactions of the audience. Teenagers ask, "Why do you have to use protection when your husband is already infected?" Health care workers want to know what your T-cell count is and what medications you are on.

Deidre's office walls are covered with thank-you notes, banners, pictures and cards from students and teachers throughout the state. She has told me that anyone speaking about HIV/AIDS must be willing to hear all types of questions, but speakers do not have to answer questions that are too personal or asked in a belittling manner. I have learned a lot from her and admire her courage. She has spoken publicly when it was obvious she was very ill.

Last night, I was asked to sit on Nashville Cares' client services board. When asked, the first thing I thought of was Deidre's advice. I've been out on sick leave since February 15.

March 1, 1995   I went to see Bev at 3 Cs today. We talked about my hands and the tests she had previously run. The tests indicate peripheral neuropathy, which would account for the numbness in my hands and feet. I told her that it's more than that, but she said that that would be the diagnosis until further tests can be run. She is sending me to a neurologist for tests. Beverly does not think the problem is peripheral neuropathy, because my T-cell count (600) is not low enough for neuropathies. (The government's definition of AIDS is a T-cell count of 200 or below.) I am glad that I was finally able to get her to listen to me, because my hands and feet warrant some investigation.

March 11, 1995 / Idea   I've been thinking for a few weeks that the stories of others need to be told, so I have decided to make a video about HIV-positive women and their families. Women will tell how they have coped, what treatments they have found useful and what effects HIV has had on their families. I know it is a big task; however, I know I will not be alone. We were all put here for a reason. There is a beginning; a middle, which is the reason; and then there is the end, which is your reward. Well, I am in the reason stage of my life. Many of us go through life having no idea, no clue, what our reason for being on earth is. That's sad. One thing I can give back is the only thing I have — myself.

The stigma associated with being HIV-positive and having AIDS must cease so that we can go about the business of treatments and cures, the business of living. This stand is very important to me, because HIV has touched my life, HIV has touched my children's lives. It will touch the lives of my future grandchildren. I want it to touch their lives in a much more positive manner.

March 13, 1995 / Neurologist's Report   I don't have carpal tunnel or peripheral neuropathy, according to this specialist's report. I asked why my hands hurt, and the neurologist told me that it was a complication of having a hysterectomy. I was not asked if I was on any hormone replacement medication. I know how my hands feel. I am so tired of fighting with doctors. This doctor was more interested in how I became HIV-positive than why my hands hurt. He also talked about his wife teaching one of those "gay young men." He said that it was a shame that the young boy chose the life he led. I could tell that this doctor had a problem with HIV-positive people. I told him I am heterosexual, and his comment was, "Well, we shouldn't make light of it." I told him I am not making light of anything and that we are talking about my life, not someone else. All I know is my hands hurt. They wake me up at night.

March 14, 1995　Aaron and Jalyon have been helping me with the new flower garden in front of the house. I have so much pain when I try to dig, so they offered to help. I have been reading about peripheral neuropathy. It is a disturbance in the peripheral nervous system, which has thirty-one pairs of nerves that connect the spinal column to the rest of the body. Some of the nerves connect the brain with our ability to smell, taste, hear and see. I'm looking forward to my appointment with the second neurologist Beverly has arranged for me to see. After my report to her, she told me that she will never send a patient to that first neurologist again.

March 20, 1995　Yesterday was wonderful for the children and me. We went to the new church we've started attending since my horrible experience with the priest. Breakfast at Shoney's, and then on to Centennial Park. The part of the day I enjoyed the most was the late-night conversation we had about God. The kids asked questions about the Bible, and I enjoyed listening to them. I felt close to all of them. Jalyon told her brothers about angels and shared the talk she and I had had. Brandon was reluctant to talk at first but soon chimed in with big-brother comments and questions. Aaron and I meditated later that evening.

Tim's working seven days a week, so the kids and I are spending lots of time together away from the house while he is sleeping.

March 22, 1995　Tim got the results of his test today. His T-cell count is down from 500 to 300. We were both devastated.

The first video meeting went well. Gwen, Donna, Lisa, Nina, Irene and Roxanne came. I was disappointed that Deidre couldn't come. Donna brought her daughter and Lisa brought her son. My kids did a great job looking after them.

The women and I talked about what we want to see in the video. We want the video to cover the women's issues that are going unaddressed. They stayed at my house until about 8:00. Everyone took home a copy of the baseline script to think about. They are going to call me tomorrow before 3:00 so I can make the changes before I see Susan at 5:30. I feel good about doing this video and will not let Tim discourage me. The women feel good about my taking on such a big task. They want to help and are very encouraging. I know this is the right thing to do. I trust God and the fact that He has put this in my heart to do. I will do this video. It will be great. It will touch people. The more I get into it, the more important this video becomes to me. I dream of what will come after this video and where this video will take me.

Later the same evening, 11:30 P.M. Having the women here has made me think about what is becoming of our group, WORTH. The group has meant so much to me and has saved my butt several times. Since the beginning, we have operated on our own, but now Nashville Cares has assigned a facilitator to our group. This makes me mad.

March 23, 1995 Up at dawn to revise the script. Sometimes I am filled with so much hope as I think of things to add to the script. I meet with Susan today. I am excited about moving forward.

Met with Susan and a student of hers named Calvin. We decided to make the video one hour long and in black and white. We are working on who will do the taping and how we will get the money.

In the middle of all this I keep thinking of the illness itself. HIV/AIDS has become the driving force behind me doing this video. I would be working at the plant and going on with my life if Tim and I were not infected by this virus. Has HIV/AIDS taken over in a new way for me? It's not just my face or Tim's face anymore. Now it includes my friends' faces and the thousands of other faces I haven't met, the global face. I am going to work on this project as long as we can keep the house going and the bills paid. I told Susan that I am pressed for time and money. If I need to make money from this, I am willing to sell it, but I would rather give it away. I would like to make enough to cover expenses and some pocket money, but it is more important to give this as a gift to those who need it. I have support from most everyone I have spoken with. Money, quality videotape and a writer are what we need. I am writing scenes, and that is hard work. Calvin is willing to help with the writing. I don't mean to sound selfish, but I envisioned doing another video after this one. I envisioned making money from this one. I envisioned making life-changing improvements for myself and my children. I am not sure how much longer Tim can work, and I wanted this to help when that happens. I listen to him tell me how his body is acting, and it worries me. He is having lots of stomach problems and has lost weight. His T-cell count is down, and from what Gwen has told me, her husband went through the same thing before he died of MAC. I worry so about Tim.

The kids have been out of school for spring break all week.

March 25, 1995   Tim took Aaron to see a four-wheeler. Brandon lost his second soccer game.

Tim and I went to Prime Cut for dinner. We talked about our Alaska trip that we took last summer. We talked about being in Gatlinburg and the great memories there. We walked around downtown's 2nd Avenue remembering the other times we had been there, looking in shop windows and people watching. Tim is still having HIV-related stomach problems, and we talked about that as well. I think we are trying that normal thing my mother recommended.

My hands still hurt, but I try not to think about them.

March 26, 1995   Lisa and I contiue to be close. She hasn't been coming to group and I miss her there, but we still have that special bond of HIV. She is still WORTH.

March 27, 1995   Picked Brandon up from school for a doctor's appointment.

March 28, 1995   Things with the video are moving slowly. There's so much to learn. I told Tim that I spend more than ten hours a day doing or thinking of things to incorporate into it.

Went to the doctor today. Bev said that I was doing great. I told her that I feel good, other than my hands. No tests were run. I am glad.

I talked to Susan. She is going to make a phone call to see if she can get someone to help with the video equipment we need. Susan is dedicated to helping make this video successful. She is a dear friend with a determined spirit. Together we will succeed. It is moving slowly, but it is moving. California backed out, but we can tape the conference in Nashville on April 7.

Midnight: note to my children   Has anybody told you today that
you are a true blessing? If not, consider it said, because you are.

March 29, 1995   Karen Moore, a friend from Meharry Medical
College, has heard about the video. She suggested that I contact a
man named Donny who has done videos for Meharry. She thinks
that he will do some of the videotaping and help with editing.

Donny and I spoke on the phone, and he agreed to donate his
talents to the project. Our first taping will be April 7. We will tape
parts of the conference that will be at the Crown Plaza Hotel in
downtown Nashville.

March 30, 1995   This day one year ago, I had surgery. Today
I feel the surgery still. The pain is still there. The scar has not
healed. My ability to stay active is limited. Over the past year, I
have learned that I must listen to my body.

I have felt down because of the date. To me, it is the beginning
of the life-changing experience I have had with HIV. I don't look
forward to April 12. I think of April 12 often and have discussed
it with Tim.

Left a message for Susan to update her on the video.

April 3, 1995   The children need clothes, the house needs painting,
but there is never enough left over to pay for such things. I am on
the front line with bills and everything else pertaining to the house
and its upkeep. I'm still on sick leave and I'm worried about it.

Saw our family attorney. He said that Tim and I did a good job
making out our wills.

April 5, 1995   Saw Joan at 8:00, after which I met Calvin at
the International House of Pancakes. He looked over the scenes I
had written. He wants to get a proposal together for a business
plan. I had no idea what an undertaking this video would be.
Scenes, scripts, business plans. This video will not have a script.
Its participants will share their experiences. No detailed script is
needed for that. Calvin thinks that I should wait until I have the
backing of the business plan before I begin. I told him that I
won't wait.

Met Tim for lunch at International Market and Restaurant. It was good. After leaving him, I met Nina at Cares, and she went to the doctor with me. We were there from 2:00 until after 6:00 P.M. After lots of tests, examinations and questions, Dr. Susskind, a neurologist, said that the problem with my hands is due to a central nervous system disorder. She said that the pain can be controlled by medication and that I should consider not going back to the plant. That worries me. I'm scheduled to return to work in July. Dr. Susskind gave me a ton of prescriptions and wants me back in a month. She wants me to remain on sick leave and have Bev call her tomorrow. All the information she gave me has not sunk in, and I need time to think about what she said. She has me scheduled for an MRI next week. I'm going to read about the central nervous system and educate myself. I was glad Nina was with me. I need time to think. It was a very busy day.

April 7, 1995 / Crown Plaza Hotel, Nashville   I arrived early and set up the video equipment with Donny. Debbie Runion was an excellent speaker. She talked about the impact HIV has had in her life and the lives of her adult children. Debbie, a journalist and college professor, referred to her doctor as Jesus Christ's brother. That is a great tribute to the doctor. Doctors are the ones that so many of us depend on for survival, education, medications and life itself.

Hank Meyers, another speaker, must unquestionably be a close relative to Christ. He deals with HIV/AIDS every day at 3 Cs. He is the chaplain. Tim and I have had his counsel. Hank spoke about HIV from a caregiving perspective. He spoke with sincerity, compassion, experience. He has attended many funerals of people who have died of AIDS. He spoke about his concern for the future. He talked of patients being carried into the clinic by family and loved ones. He spoke of the injustice and humiliation. He spoke of the loss and grief. I stood at the back and cried as he spoke.

April 9, 1995   As I think about what's going on with my hands and feet, I get scared. A central nervous system problem is a big problem. I have read several books and articles on HIV and the nervous system. Tim has, too. Seems as though this disease has power. It shows up in every body differently and manages to slap me into recognizing it.

It's a heavy feeling, an alone feeling, a selfish feeling, often asking, "Why me? What did I do wrong to deserve this?" Wishing things could be different. Wanting life to be different. When and, more important, how will it end?

I would like my story told as a learning tool. Whether HIV is contracted by having unprotected sex, using needles or having blood transfusions, this is no way to live. I don't want to die.

April 12, 1995   Couldn't write.

April 13, 1995   Results are back from neurological tests. MRI is normal. Doctor's report says central nervous system disorder. Each person's body is different, and HIV enters into the body and settles in different places throughout the body. I have learned that HIV first settles in the central nervous system and then spreads. I still read most everything I can, as often as I can. I go to the library and have read everything there. I will have to wait and see what Bev says now.

My brother Melvin and Mom got in about 5:00. The kids were happy. We didn't do much after eating, just sat around and talked.

Nashville Cares' newsletter printed my poem. I am proud of myself.

I think Tim has been drinking. I am not surprised, nor are the kids.

April 14, 1995   Tim and I brought home a small potbelly pig. Her name is Thai Shea Nanning. She is quiet and everyone loves her.

April 15, 1995   Slow day. Tim and my brother took the kids to the arcade. My mother and I went riding in the country. We talked a little about what the doctor has said but not much more. She still thinks that prayer will make it go away.

April 16, 1995   Easter was slow. We had a big family dinner. Tim continues to drink.

April 18, 1995   Melvin and Mother are gone and had a safe trip back.

The work on the video is going very well. Tim is OK with it now that he is involved. Brandon is changing before my very eyes. I see a young man beginning to take form.

April 20, 1995   Trying not to think about myself is getting more difficult. My hands, lower back, feet and stomach are constantly hurting.

April 24, 1995   I told Brandon and Aaron about what HIV is doing to my body these days. Brandon was quiet, as usual, and Aaron had questions, as usual. I told them about the central nervous system and how the virus has caused the pain in my hands, arms, legs and feet. We still haven't told Jalyon yet. It just doesn't seem like the right time.

Bev's diagnosis is peripheral neuropathy caused by HIV. She recommends the pain clinic for now.

Been working on summer camps for the children.

Aaron and I found a four-wheeler and are waiting for Tim to go look at it.

April 26, 1995   Tim and I went to look at the four-wheeler. The man gave Tim the same price as he gave me: $1,899. Too much money for a used four-wheeler.

The video is still in the wait mode. Haven't heard from Susan yet. Haven't heard from Atlanta yet.

Saw Joan today. Asked her what she thinks of my mental progress. She feels that I am doing fine with the things in my life and sees me progressing through difficult things like the situation at the plant, advancing HIV/AIDS, neuropathy, a husband who drinks, and a mother who can't accept HIV right now.

Joan wants me to bring Thai, the pig, to the next session. Jalyon wants me to bring Thai to school, so I told her that I would bring her this Friday. We took her with us today downtown and to the pet store. She does pretty good in the back of the Camaro.

April 28, 1995   For several weeks now, Nina and the other women from group have been telling me about a mushroom tea they are drinking. I am interested because the medication the neurologist gave me has not helped my hands and the side effects are awful.

Still working on the video. The video is not moving, and I am getting a little worried. Nothing from Susan. Atlanta has backed out.

Thai is doing great. The family loves her, and she is growing fast. I am taking her to Jalyon's school tomorrow. That will make her happy.

May 1, 1995   Tim's working eight days in a row, so he will be pretty grouchy before it's over. My hands are still bothering me, and the pain seems to be getting worse. It moves up my arms, especially my left arm.

I still enjoy writing. I am talking more with the kids about the things I am writing, because they need to be educated. Brandon is studying about HIV/AIDS in school. I hope he is listening.

May 4, 1995   Dr. Susskind told me that I have HIV myelopathy, which is a central nervous system disorder that affects the spinal cord. Dr. Susskind was very careful to tell me that it in no way affects my brain. Having a name to put on the pain is somewhat of a relief. HIV has entered my body, settled itself in my spinal cord and is now causing the pain. Now the doctor wants me to take eight to ten amitriptyline a night, after which she will give me another pill to keep the pain slight. Tim and I talked about what she said. He knows that I don't want to take any medication. I want to go to the pain clinic that Bev advised me to try. I am trying to be receptive to as much information and advice as possible.

Tim took the night off, and we went for a long drive. On the way home, he got a traffic ticket. His driver's license was taken because of an earlier unpaid traffic ticket.

Thai has become an important part of the family. I take her places like soccer games, the pet store and Nashville Cares.

May 12, 1995   Tim feels sick and doesn't want to know what his T-cell count is. He doesn't want to see Bev. His eyes are bothering him. He's told me before how his vision gets blurry, but it is getting worse. He has a hard time reading the paper and keeping his vision focused. His arms have gotten worse. Mowing the lawn hurts him. His stomach has not gotten any better, and some days he's fixed to the toilet. Now his vision is getting worse and I don't know what to do. I want to tell Bev, but that won't make him go see her. He just keeps working. He comes home and drops or cries. He's been on AZT for a while now and needs to be reevaluated. I told him that it's time to ask Bev about other things, but he won't see her now. I hope I can get him to see her soon.

The family went to Aaron's school play last night. Tim and I had tears in our eyes as we watched. We seem to look at everything with more emotion these days, trying to soak up every moment of our children's activities. We are so proud. It's great to see them in soccer and in plays at school. All my children are so much alike and yet so different.

May 14, 1995 / Mother's Day   The children gave me cards, and Tim brought the perfume I wanted. We went riding in the country and stopped to read some historical signs. Tim fixed juicy homemade hamburgers for dinner. We ate corn on the cob and watermelon. It was a wonderful day. I don't know how many Mother's Days I have left, so this one was special. When I was first diagnosed, I was told that I had six years, so I guess it's down to five. In five years Brandon will be eighteen, Aaron will be seventeen and Jalyon fourteen, so I have to pack all the mothering I can into every day.

May 16, 1995   Tim got up this morning, got dressed, kissed me good-bye, went downstairs, sat on the couch and could not move. When he doesn't go to work, I can bet something's wrong. When I went downstairs later, I was surprised to see him. He told me that he just didn't have the energy to go. I was concerned yesterday when he didn't go to work, but today it's more than concern. He's been feverish for weeks. His color has been off, too. He's not eating much, and his stomach still bothers him.

After he rested for a long time, I took him to get his license. He didn't pass the eye test. He couldn't see the letters in the machine. His eyes are worse than he has said. He can't keep them focused, and things get all jammed together. As he was trying to read the letters, everyone in the room got quiet. He stammered trying to read them but could not focus. His eyes have always been better than mine, and he used to brag about how he could see better than me. The lady behind the counter told him to go to an eye doctor and bring the results back. He came home and laid back down.

He wanted so much to take the boys to a group at Vanderbilt that he goes to on Tuesday nights. This group has come to mean a lot to him. The young people in this support group are there for running away, drug or alcohol abuse, child abuse and other reasons. He's gone to several of these Tuesday evening meetings since he was first asked a few months ago. His outreach is about HIV, drug abuse and the dangers of each. He was supposed to chair this meeting tonight and wanted to take his sons. He was too sick to go. He talked about it all day, wanting to feel better so that he could go. He said, "HIV sucks." He has been stressing over his license since it was taken the night we went riding. Not passing the eye test today has him stressing more. I am very worried about my husband. He wanted me to stay close to him, so I didn't do the things I had planned. He wants to feel better so we can go away next weekend for the holiday. We are supposed to go camping. He said, "I hope I feel better next week so we can go." I told him that he will and that everything will be all right.

May 18, 1995   Took Tim to the doctor — a different one. He told us that he didn't think it was CMV (cytomegalovirus), which we thought it was. I told the doctor that Tim's T-cell count has continued to drop since he has been taking AZT. He agreed after reading the chart. The doctor also told Tim about the ills of drinking. He showed him a spot on his arm that indicates liver damage. Oh, how I wish Tim didn't drink. He ordered blood work and told Tim that he needs to start thinking about adding a different medication to the AZT.

Tim's been lying down all day but says he feel better. I can only hope that the doctor was right, because if it is CMV, it has to be dealt with fast or he could lose his eyesight. I am not convinced and will feel better when the blood work's back. I called our parents in Michigan.

My mother is extremely worried and said that she's been thinking about us for days. She told me that she's lived seventy years and would change places with us if she could. I said that we need her prayers. She said, "You got all my prayers." She claimed not to be in denial, and she thinks about what we are faced with every day of her life. She wants to trade places with us because we are so young. We both were crying by then, and I just kept telling her, "I need you to love me. I need you to be with me. I need you to pray for us." She loves her son-in-law and is concerned about both of us.

I called Tim's mother and told her that he hadn't passed his eye test at the license bureau and how he has been lying around. She began to cry. She was grateful I called her, because she wants to know what is going on with her son. She knows that he doesn't tell her everything when they talk. His mom said that it goes against the laws of nature for a parent to bury a child and how this phone call has given her a wake-up call to face whatever might happen to both of us. I told her that we are not sure what it is, but the doctor said it wasn't CMV.

Right now, my only concern is Tim and making sure that he is treated with whatever is necessary for him to get better. I hope it's only old age and he gets glasses and everything is fine, but that does not explain the nausea, fever, fatigue and sudden loss of vision.

Bad storms today — fifty-six tornados sighted; three people killed.

May 20, 1995   Aaron's out-of-school party was a great success. More kids showed up than expected. He'd been bumming all week, talking about only two or three kids showing. He had nine, including Chris, a girl in his class he likes. Water balloon fights, soda, silly string, chips and basketball set the agenda for fun.

Irene called. She and her seven-year-old daughter are both positive. Irene is in the hospital with a 105-degree temperature and a shadow on her lung. A few months ago, she was in the hospital with one of those long-named illnesses. She was at death's door then, but she came home. She was doing fine until last night. Her T-cell count was forty-nine two months ago, but she doesn't know what it is now. The hospital drew her labs, and she will know soon. Irene said that she feels "like shit," whipped and fatigued, wanting to move but having no energy. Who does that sound like? When I got off the phone, I called my telephone tree partner. Everyone in group will know by morning.

It's been a few days since Tim first woke up and told me, "Honey, I don't feel well." Today he is experiencing vomiting, nausea, fever and blurred vision and he says, "I feel like someone has reached inside me and is pulling me down." His body seems to be working overtime to keep him upright, because with a little push he could fall over. He sleeps a lot, and in his waking hours he is mean. The inner anger he has always had seems to be intensifying. His skin seems flushed all the time, like it is when he has been drinking. Tim has always had a self-hatred that has shown itself many times in the past. I think it's part of the constant fight he has with alcohol. Now it shows itself because he feels sick all the time. He doesn't like feeling so bad, and another opportunity of self-hatred is taking over. He has been drinking today, I can still tell. *I can always tell.*

When he got home tonight, he came running in saying that he had just vomited all over himself and the front seat of the truck. I wanted to go and help him clean it up. He insisted on cleaning it up himself. Later I looked in the truck and found empty beer bottles under the front seat. I think he had been drinking all day; finding the bottles just confirmed it.

I feel that I am on a slow death with him. Sometimes I wish it would all end. He knows what this is doing to him, and so do I. If he wants to drink himself to death, I wish he would and get it over. I find myself grieving for him already, and he is not dead. Living grief, watching him die, unable to do anything, helpless in attempts to make him stop. I think that he wants to die and this is the only way he has to speed it up. He really does hate himself. It is taking its toll on me. Living with an HIV/AIDS alcoholic is devastatingly hard.

My friends want to know how I handle it. I don't know. I think of my children and try to stay focused. Some days I can't take care of myself and shut down.

May 22, 1995 I think I'm going to call Susan today and tell her to forget about the video. I have had four people lined up, but no production has started. I'm feeling pretty low these days, because nothing is going right. My life is in a holding pattern that I can do nothing about. My marriage is empty, the video is empty, my work situation is empty and I am empty. Irene, Roxanne, Debbie and Tim are all sick.

May 26, 1995   Susan is leaving the country Sunday and will be returning in a month. Calvin is also leaving the country, and I don't think he will be coming back to Nashville, so I will be alone to work on the video. That's OK with me. I just hope I get someone to commit.

Brandon and Aaron got scholarships to Camp Marymount at the end of summer. Now I want to find something for them to do between the end of school next week and going to camp in late July. Jalyon is all set for Girl Scout camp.

May 30, 1995   The camping trip was hard on me.

Tomorrow is payday and I haven't received my check stub. I wonder what the trouble is.

I went to see Nina today. She's moving to New York tomorrow. We have become good friends since we met in group three months ago. Nina said that she didn't like support groups, because she would become attached to people and they would move away or forget about those whose lives they touched or die. She and I became close and talked on the phone often. She gave me the recipe for mushroom tea and other information on nutrition she has used over the ten years she's been HIV-positive. I thanked her again for going to the neurologist with me. We intend to keep in touch by phone and letters.

May 31, 1995   Tim's gone to take the eye test again so he can get his license. He was troubled. He is concerned that he may not pass it again. With all that is going on with my check (it still hasn't come), we are both worried. Then there's my health. Seems it stays in last place until I can't get up.

Rely on your faith. It will be tested.

June 2, 1995   Went to the plant to get my check.

Irene's been out of the hospital for a few days. Her elderly mother has been watching over her daughter, little Deondra. AIDS has been hard on their family. Deondra has been too sick to attend school regularly. She was born with the virus and has never had a well day in her seven years. Irene contracted HIV at age fourteen after a blood transfusion when she broke her neck. HIV was not discovered until she was six months pregnant.

June 3, 1995   The family went to the open house at Girl Scout camp in Ashland City. My mother had sent money for tennis shoes for Brandon. Aaron brought a guitar, and Jalyon got some things for camp. It's good my mother is helping with the kids.

June 4, 1995   It's late and Tim just left the room, but the aroma of alcohol remains. I remain suffering in silence. As I protect myself from the pain of his addiction, I am comforted by faith — faith that things have to get better. Without counseling, I can no longer hold out much hope for my marriage. I am not an active participant in my marriage anymore. No longer is my voice heard. My walls of security are high, and the valley between us is very wide.

June 5, 1995   Had lunch with Deidre. It was good to spend time with her.
    I told Tim that we need counseling. His response was, "Do I care?" I told him that I am suggesting counseling *because I care*. "If we go to counseling, you'll make the appointment." His response was "fuck that." I am in too much physical pain to let his words hurt me. I am drained of any strength.

June 6, 1995   I've been having massage therapy every two weeks since the neurologist told me about myelopathy. It's part of the health regimen she suggested in addition to the medications. Julie, the massage therapist, told me that the muscles in my back were very tight. My back muscles tightened more as she worked on me. The pain in my hands is still happening and I wouldn't let her touch them.

June 8, 1995   Tim and I had a counseling session. We needed it badly. He's still not back to work, and finances are tight.
    No word regarding the video. I am concerned about that.

June 9, 1995 / Another Dream   After a long day of running everybody everywhere, I fell into bed around 10. Tim complained that I was snoring, so I went across the hall to sleep. I had a dream I want to write about. I think I was watching this dream, because there were two women and I felt that I was both of them. Anyway, there was a young black woman sitting on a bench in what looked like a park. Two young white men — one on a motorcycle, the other in a small dark car — drove up, jumped out and ran up to the woman. She knew that they would cause her pain, and she began to panic as they approached her. She tried to run, but they caught her and began taunting her. One had a knife and the other had a gun. The knife was poked at her and the gun was waved around her as they called her racist names and told her that she was going to die because she was black and did not deserve to live. She broke lose from them and ran toward the right up a dirt road to another part of the park, where there were about six or eight young black people playing and wrestling around with a basketball. As she ran toward them, she split. Part of her ran toward them, and another part of her ran toward a small dark building that looked like a bathroom. I followed the part of her that ran toward the crowd first. She was screaming and calling to the people, but they could not hear her over the music and laughter. They were playing behind parked cars with music going. The doors of the cars were open. They were having a wonderful time and thought that she was coming to join them. As she ran toward them, the ball they were playing with got away from them and began rolling toward her. She kept running toward them and grabbed the black ball, which had a red circle on both sides and yellow and white figures and writing on it. She cupped the ball, and they began to notice that she was screaming. By that time, the two men had almost reached them. She looked back and saw them coming, and as they approached, they yelled racist remarks and started shooting in the air. The one with the knife caught the woman and told her that she had to watch the others die as a punishment for escaping. She fell to the ground and tried to cover her face, but she watched as one of them drove the knife into one of the young girls and dragged it down her back. The other man shot most of the rest of them as they were running away. Blood was everywhere, and screams of pain filled the air. She lay on the ground in a state of confusion and shock. They came to her, picked her up by the hair and told her that it was her turn to die. The man with the knife slit her throat. Her body became warm as the blood began to run down the front of her. She slid down in slow motion into a clump as death took control. Then I saw the other woman who had run into the bathroom, which was in a different part of the park. She was huddled in a corner covered with blood, but I could see no wounds. She was shaking, crying and taking off what looked like gloves, but there was no hand covering, just fingers. She took one finger glove covering off, then another and another. This woman was the original one who was sitting on the bench reading when the men approached. This dream was so strange to me. I told Joan, and she suggested that I write it.

"If any of you lacks wisdom, he should ask God, who gives generously to all without finding fault, and it will be given to him" (James 1:5).

June 10, 1995   The twelve-step approach to life is just for today. Sometimes things come upon me, and living in a twenty-four-hour time frame becomes too much. Living in the moment is the best I can do. Telling myself I am OK right now is all I can say, at times. I am still in a hurried state. Having to hurry and tell the children what they should know is still a big part of my writings. Knowing that they are children makes it seem unfair that they should listen in detail to every word I say. It is children's nature not to listen to their parents. But we can only hope that eventually they do listen. Raising children in the 1990s!

June 12, 1995   More problems. I feel that I am being mistreated by the company and my union brothers.

June 16, 1995   Jalyon's been at camp for a week. We're to pick her up tomorrow. We look forward to that.

Brandon, Aaron and I spent the morning shopping for Father's Day gifts. We found a beautiful dream catcher. Tim has always wanted one. Maybe I should have gotten one for me. I had a good time. We were all stupid, and it was fun. Family Dollar and Walmart are where we acted like nuts.

June 18, 1995   Jalyon's home from camp, sick. Tim and I were so happy to see her, we talked all the way home until she fell asleep in the backseat of the truck.

June 20, 1995 / Afflictions of HIV/AIDS   I've given thought to myelopathy. I haven't found much information, but I will continue the search. It's rare, and I was told that I have progressive myelopathy, whatever that means. Last night I had what I call a fit. My arms and legs were moving uncontrollably. I managed to get out of bed and walk the floor trying to stop it. I fell asleep in the other room. I woke up this morning and couldn't remember where I was. I had gone to sleep in one room, woke in another and didn't remember.

Later, I went out to pay a bill and felt strange driving. I feel a little disoriented and unsure of myself. I get a funny feeling and a strange taste in my mouth at times. I have been feeling that way for about a week. I don't want to read more into this than there is, but I can't help wondering what is happening to me. I tried telling Tim my concerns, but he said, "You can't let anything go, can you?" I will not discuss my concerns with him again. I wish he had gone back to work. Our relationship is about the same. We just can't seem to get close anymore. One form of HIV or another is always around to come between us. I love Tim; I just can't love him closely anymore. That's sad, isn't it?

June 23, 1995 / Seizure   The morning of June 22 was like any other morning. I planned a full day with the boys, because Jalyon was in summer day camp and would be gone all day. The boys and I started out our morning going to Nashville Cares to pick up a letter recommending me to serve on the Tennessee HIV/AIDS Community Prevention Planning Group. I don't remember driving there, but later I was told that we had been there about ten minutes before I had the seizure. I had asked the boys if they wanted sodas, and I remember walking with Brandon to the soda machine to get them and walking back. I had called my mother long distance, which I don't remember doing, and I talked to her and handed the phone to Aaron. I don't remember anything else, but Aaron said that I began to shake uncontrollably and fell from the chair to the floor, where I bit my tongue and wet my pants. Aaron began to scream for help. People came running in, and someone called 911. Brandon was on the phone with his grandma, and she would not let him get off. I don't remember anything else until I opened my eyes in an ambulance and found a strange man telling me that I was going to be OK. I spent the next few hours in the emergency room at Southern Hills Hospital.

When I came to, Tim was standing over me telling me where I was and that the boys were OK. My first concern was that I could have hurt them if I had been driving. I cried a long time. Tim kept trying to comfort me, but I still cried. I can only imagine how hard the whole thing was for my boys to watch, not knowing what to do or what was wrong with me. I am sorry they had to see this happen. I don't ever want to hurt them, and I thank God I was not driving. Had it been fifteen minutes earlier, we would have been on I-65. My only thought was my sons, not hurting my sons. Tim said that I kept saying, "The boys, the boys, I could have hurt the boys." He kept saying, "But you didn't, they're all right, Catherine." Confused and scared, I held Tim's hand and drifted in and out of consciousness.

The emergency room doctor admitted me after talking to Dr. Susskind. Several hours later, I woke up in my hospital room still confused, disoriented, scared, in pain from biting my tongue and sleepy. I slept well into the night. I woke up a few times during the night confused and crying. In the morning, I realized that a sign on my door said: "Blood and body fluids contaminated, use precautions." Nothing like this has ever happened to me, and the shock of it still scares me.

This afternoon brought more tests and more confusion. When Tim walked in with the children, I was grateful all over again. Finally at the end of the day, Dr. Susskind came in and told me I could go home.

June 25, 1995   As I laid in my hospital bed, my mind kept repeating, it's time for Jalyon to know. It's no longer an option keeping secrets from my little girl. She has every right to be told the truth.

Tim drove the boys to the halfway point between Tennessee and Michigan. My mother met them. I had been planning to drive them, but plans changed after I had the seizure. The trip was good for Tim and Jalyon. It gave them time to talk and work on their relationship.

June 26, 1995 / Telling Jalyon Tim was out of the house, and the boys were safe in Michigan with their grandmother. I had not been allowed out of bed by the doctors. It was a quiet Sunday afternoon, and Jalyon and I lay together. I felt that it was a good time to tell her. Using some of the same pictures Tim and I had shared with the boys, I told her that Dad and I are HIV-positive. She wanted to know what HIV is. My chance to educate my daughter was at hand, and I took full advantage without going overboard. I told her that it is the virus that causes AIDS, showing her the pictures. "But we don't have AIDS," I said, and she was fine with that. She asked if she has HIV, because Aaron had accidentally stuck her with a needle while he was in the hospital two years ago with tonsillitis. Reassuringly, I said, "No." I told her that the three of them had been tested shortly after her father and I had been diagnosed. I also told her, with a heavy heart, the importance of keeping this from her friends. She understood. "If you have any questions, Jalyon, ask."

"OK, Mama, I will."

"I love you, Jalyon."

"I know, Mama, I love you too. Were you in the hospital because of HIV?"

"Yes, Jalyon, I was."

"Will you and Daddy be all right, Mama?"

"Yes, baby, Daddy and I will be fine."

"Good, Mama."

I continued reading to her about HIV and explaining the pictures we were looking at. Telling her wasn't as bad as I had imagined it would be. She promised to come to me with any more questions, and we soon left the subject. Shortly afterward, she fell asleep beside me. I lay watching her, wishing desperately that I could live to see her become a woman. Now everyone who is important in my life knows, and I feel less burdened by secrets. I hated keeping this secret from Jalyon for so long.

Tim was disappointed that I told her without his being there, but the timing was appropriate. Tim and I are now free to speak openly in our home about the virus that haunts us. I am so glad she finally knows. I hated carrying around the secret.

June 27, 1995   Tim took me to have an EEG, a type of brain scan. Dr. Susskind wanted to repeat these tests because of the seizure. She read the results while we waited. It was a long day. I was very tired, because I was allowed to get only four hours' sleep before the test. The test did not show why I had the seizure, but Dr. Susskind had not expected it to. She put me on a seizure medication, because the chance of recurrence is great. I don't feel good about the possibility that this could happen again. I'm not embarrassed about what happened to me at Nashville Cares, but I do wonder about my ability to drive.

June 30, 1995   Two days before the seizure, I had been feeling disoriented, but only for a short time. I was unable to make sense or speak clearly. I couldn't remember phone numbers, PIN numbers or my address. I blew off all these things in passing and ignored every sign.

Tomorrow night I return to work. It was not easy convincing Dr. Susskind to let me return. I'm dealing with pain in my hands, wrists and arms, still.

2:00 A.M.   I feel angry at God for not listening to my prayers. I prayed for the freedom, time and energy to work on His calling for my life, but nothing, except a seizure, has happened to ease this worry for me. I have asked God to walk with me through all my problems, but again I feel alone and angry. Is it wrong to be angry at God? Are people supposed to get angry at God? It is not what I was taught in Catholic school or in the Catholic Church. Is it that my faith is small and God doesn't hear me? I wish I knew what to do.

The seizure taught me that life can be gone in an instant, and time is really short. My mission — the video — has not progressed for some time. The only footage we have is what we shot at the Crown Plaza. Agencies and people keep backing out because I have no money. The cost of making a video is astronomical. We are barely making ends meet at home, so I can't afford to pay anyone for their time or equipment. I have spent the evening talking to God, asking Him to surround me with His power.

Jalyon, Brandon, and Aaron.

July 1, 1995 Brandon and Aaron have been in Michigan since June 25, having a great time with family. Jalyon's doing her summer camp thing. I got a friend to stay with Jalyon tonight, while I went back to work.

Just got home from work. I could not believe how hard it was to get back in. I went to the medical department, which is the procedure to follow when returning from sick leave. The nurse was reluctant when she read the restrictions I was returning with. I have several, but the ones that got her were "limited hours" and "frequent rest periods." I looked at the nurse and said, "Lady, all the hell I have gone through to get back, oh, I'm coming back. I suggest you get someone on the phone." She got on the phone to her supervisor and came back reluctantly with a return-to-work slip. We had debated my return for over an hour.

I went to see the supervisor in charge of the area I was returning to. This area has hard, heavy jobs, and I knew that I could not do those jobs, but it was where I had to go. He looked at my restrictions and laughed. I will be in this area for a month before I can be moved. It's awful, but it's still better than the last area and supervisor.

July 4, 1995   We spent the day at an NA picnic out at the dam. It was fun. Jalyon made friends quickly, and Tim and I talked with people we knew. Afterward we came home and went downtown to watch the fireworks. They were wonderful, and the crowd was large. Tim never let me out of his sight. I enjoyed the day and the night.

July 6, 1995   The boys are back from Michigan, and the deprogramming has started. My mother brought them home and took Jalyon back with her. Tim and I will see her in three weeks when we go up.

I haven't felt well today. Yesterday I woke up with swollen glands and a sore throat. Swollen glands happen a lot.

I have been spending time in doubt, which is not a good place to be. Doubting the video's completion, doubting that Tim will stop drinking, doubting my ability to drive by myself because I may have another seizure, doubting my job security, doubting that we will get out of the financial bind we're in. Seems the more I believe things will change, the more they stay the same. I believe God's word, but I doubt I am hearing Him. I doubt that the video was a mission. Maybe it was a selfish act I came up with on my own, and it will do nothing to help anyone. Maybe I need to revisit my mission conversation with God. I know I should have patience, but maybe I was wrong from the beginning about God wanting me to do this. I am so unsure about everything else in my life, how can I be sure that God wants me to do anything?

July 10, 1995   Fran told me about her God box. A God box is a box where all the things that worry, bother and bring unhappiness are put. I will have a God box.

Fran is dating since her divorce and having a wonderful time with her life. I'm so happy for her. She deserves to be happy. She gave me a God box, just the "medicine" I needed. She will remain my friend. I started my God box today.

July 11, 1995 I got the haircut from hell.

July 12, 1995 I am so excited because it finally seems like the thing God has given me to do will get done. I had sent out a mass mailing asking for people experienced in production and documentary editing. The mailing asked for those willing to donate equipment and their talent. I received a favorable response. I have been busy calling those who are willing to be filmed and making arrangements for next Wednesday's shoot.

Susan and I met today to discuss the video. She is excited too and believes in the need for this documentary as much as I do. We strategized about length and agreed on thirty minutes. She will speak with a friend who is an actress and ask her to narrate the film.

July 14, 1995 Went to 3 Cs to get my permanent restrictions, requested by the company. This means a more restricted area, but maybe it will give me a chance to get back on my feet. The surgery is now over a year old, and I have not healed. Walking upright remains a challenge. People continue to comment. I am relieved to know that my T-cell count is still above 500. That number remains important.

July 15, 1995 Aaron and Brandon stayed home alone all day and ordered pizza, and I had rented movies for them. Jalyon is still in Michigan with Grandma. Thai is rooting everything, eating everything, growing by the hour.

July 16, 1995 Picked LaVonna up from the airport and took her home. I enjoyed talking with her again. We had lots of catching up to do, since I don't see her at work anymore. She and I used to work together and have remained friends. LaVonna has filled my head with, "Girl, don't worry about those assholes at the plant. You have to take care of yourself." She's been a confidante.

July 17, 1995   Lisa has had surgery to try to correct a chronic sinus infection. Even though she has been sick for quite some time, she has been supportive of the video and looks forward to participating. I make it my business to check up on her weekly. She's always been there for me, and I will be there for her.

July 18, 1995   Work the last few days has been hard on me. Walking drains me. I am once again in pain but trying not to walk bent over.

July 19, 1995   We began shooting the video today, and I was elated. The first shoot with Bobbi Lee and Roxanne went very well. Susan and I were very happy, but we know that this taping is just the beginning. People are talking about the video; many have seen the flyers that have been posted around town.

The company's medical director has lost the four letters I had given him. Tim and I share concern. We can't understand where they are, but we know what could happen now that they are missing. I also found out that more than the medical staff has access to employee medical files.

I am just as consumed with being HIV-positive today as I was yesterday and last year. Listening to people with this illlness lends itself a different ear. I pay close attention. Talking with women and men infected with HIV/AIDS reminds me that the faces of AIDS are many. It's not just me. Desperately I move forward, trying to keep the video rolling. To me, every delay means another infected person. Fatigue has taken me; I'm staying close to home and bed.

July 20, 1995   Since learning about the mandatory HIV testing that government officials want to conduct, many have fought a valiant fight against the implementation of ACTG 076. Mandatory testing for every American woman who becomes pregnant may seem to be harmless on paper, but in reality, it could discourage women from getting proper medical care for themselves and their unborn children. The American health care system has already failed those without insurance, and today it is rapidly taking health care from those with insurance. They didn't listen

Memories
I walk alone searching for you
Set apart from all others
We look at eyes that look at us with love.

Alone
Emptiness in my heart I take the chance of a
   lifetime.

Togetherness
One becomes more. Life changes and happiness
   is sought
Years turn into hours, clock ticks away days.

Happy
We thought forever would last forever.
Reminiscence, you are no longer here and I am
   alone once again.

Wondering
I give this to you with love and heartfelt insight.

to those without insurance who have cried for help for years. Now it's middle America's turn to be at the mercy of members of the House and Senate, all of whom have insurance and benefits for themselves.

I am so saddened by all the bureaucracy AIDS has brought. AIDS walks bring in billions of dollars for what? Research. Comedy personalities and actors wear red ribbons neatly perched on expensive attire as they accept awards for outstanding performances. Has wearing an AIDS ribbon become a fad?

Realizing that the Cancer Society would be out of business if a cure were found might help with understanding, but it doesn't cut it for me. I am still positive and still wanting answers about what's up with all the paperwork.

I now sit on the Tennessee HIV Prevention Community Planning Group and listen to the opinions of persons without the virus. I listen to those with the virus speak, and their tones fill the air and touch my core. Policy setting should include more HIV/AIDS-positive people. Policies regarding HIV/AIDS education, health, research and care facilities should be based on the input of more persons living with the virus.

While maneuvering forward on the making of the video, I'm learning fast why African Americans (black people, my personal preference) have been reluctant to take ownership of the epidemic that lives within our community. I hope to convince all minorities that what may seem crazy and "going public" can save lives. If I'm right, there is a profound need to reorient and educate ourselves and our children so that we can all succeed in a multicultural society.

Health officials can't just wander into the local inner-city neighborhood with pamphlets, goodwill and condoms and expect people to listen. Nor can they influence minority corporations with big, frightening words of despair and expect behaviors to change. Every American has some risk-behavior potential. We are losing our sons and daughters at a tremendous rate. Resistance within the community has ranged from simple refusal to acknowledge the virus — denial — to rejection of programs designed for minorities, which in some cases is understandable. We talk about it as little as possible and rarely involve ourselves in efforts aimed at

The Ribbon

The mailman brought word.
Playgrounds were once filled with laughter
four square, hide an' seek, basketball, jump rope.
Moms in the kitchen, boys ruff and tumble.
Seasons changed, the ground turned savage
Cap guns turn kill guns.
Ring around the rosy, now we all do fall down
Rainbows of ribbon released in midair
Red, yellow, blue, purple.
Those lost to ill, those lost in pain.
Humpty Dumpty fell off the wall, heart disease
    cracked his fall
Little Sally Walker has taken up her soccer
Mary's little lamb became beast
Cancer ribbons are common just don't ask
    Pinocchio
Romeo infected Juliet.
Ribbons, symbols worn by grief-stricken ones
ribbon in the hair no more
ribbons in the heart for sure
Little Ms. Muffet no longer sits on her tuffet, the
    curds and whey are now ribboned.
Jack and Jill caught that mental ill, now
    Rock-a-bye-baby's doin' smack.
enee menee miney moe, herpes is it Rapunzel
    said so.
Balloons did hover, fields of flowers were the
    cover.
Trees bear ribbons, poles bear ribbons,
our souls bear ribbons.

The mailman brought word yesterday.

a solution. Unquestionably, the virus is hitting the black community hardest, like most things do, due to economic woes. I don't think we can afford to continue to allow race to be a factor that causes our children any more misery. Quite simply, we as a people should stop talking past one another and begin to listen twice as much.

July 21, 1995   I read today that according to the CDC, 43 percent of women over the age of sixty-five with AIDS die within one month of diagnosis due to lack of education about HIV/AIDS and also due to the belief that it could not happen to them. Sadly, I continued to read that this group of women is now acquiring HIV/AIDS through heterosexual contact, not just through transfusions. Midlife women tend to think that their symptoms are old age or menopausal changes. Older women are having unprotected sex just like their younger counterparts, but their generation feels far removed from HIV/AIDS. How can we reach them and explain that it can happen to them? Could you tell your mother or grandmother to practice safe sex? The old way of not thinking or talking about sex, which that generation harbors, has to stop. Unfortunately, the facts are that they are not removed, and they are dying at enormous rates. Old sex, young sex, any unprotected sex is unsafe.

July 22, 1995, 4:00 A.M.   The sun has not yet come up, but I could not sleep after coming home from work, so this hour of the morning finds me at the computer writing.

Tim told me, "If something unnatural doesn't happen, AIDS will," during our last conversation about HIV/AIDS. Lately, we have been hearing and reading that some experts now believe that it doesn't take HIV alone to cause AIDS. Tim really doesn't agree with that way of thinking. He feels strongly that it takes HIV in order to get AIDS and that those of us with HIV will eventually get AIDS unless a cure is found. Knowing friends who have been hospitalized with unexplained this and that or hospitalized for the same opportunistic infections (OIs) they dealt with in the past is stressful. Those of us living each day anticipating sickness often find ourselves living in a state of "wait."

My extended HIV/AIDS family has grown over the past year, and knowledge of our personal future has become clearer. There are so many things to look out for. It's not only some of those OIs I've mentioned, but it could be neuropathy, anemia or forms of cancer. There is little doubt, at least in my mind, that waiting for the next episode of HIV/AIDS in our lives has become something normal. The only question is what it will be and when it will happen. For me, life and HIV/AIDS has become that matter-of-fact.

Many of us, myself included, work at safeguarding ourselves from those discomforts by taking what is termed holistic or natural approaches; others, including Tim, choose to take traditional Western therapies. Whichever road we choose to take, we still get sick. These are stressful times. I've been told by professionals that stress is a very bad thing for the immune system — that the top priority is to cut stress. Yeah, right! It's stressful just to think about cutting stress. What does that cut out of your already shortened life? Work, family, friends, relatives and the general public are all forms of stress one way or the other — maybe not all at once, but each one can be and often is stressful. For Tim and me, the central challenge is to stay healthy, whichever way we choose. Whether it be natural or with medication, we, like my extended HIV/AIDS family, just want to be healthy enough for the next time the disease hits — different approaches to the virus that causes AIDS.

He and I know that we are fortunate to have insurance that covers our medical expenses, HIV/AIDS resources such as Nashville Cares to help, supportive friends who truly care, and an extended family of friends living with HIV/AIDS who are willing to share their lives and experiences with us. Most of all, we are blessed to have the love of our children.

With all that wonderfulness, my imagination still envisions AIDS in one form or another, one way or the other, happening to each one of us.

"If something unnatural doesn't happen, AIDS will." How many people do you know who have been hit by that proverbial bus? How many people do I know who are infected?

July 23, 1995 We took the boys to Camp Marymount today. They had waited all summer to go, and it was finally time after weeks of preparation. Packing tons of shirts, pants, shorts, swimming suits, towels and everything took time, and they still said they wouldn't have enough. I, unlike lots of parents, am saddened to see them go, but knowing that they will have a good time makes it easier. This is the first time they've gone to camp.

July 25, 1995   Tim and I are working, the boys are at camp, Jalyon's up north with Grandma. I hope the boys are doing OK and having fun. I know Jalyon is enjoying herself with her grandmother and uncle. She's told me about trips to the Detroit Zoo and outdoor concerts her uncle has taken her to. She went on and on about nights spent at her grandparents' and how much fun it's been spending time with her cousins on that side of the family. I am happy to hear the joy and excitement in her voice.

Tim and I are getting ready to go to Michigan for my family reunion. I am looking forward to seeing family I haven't seen for almost twenty years. Tim's sick. I hope he feels better soon and can make the trip feeling good and in a good mood. He has been resting in his chair a lot lately, and I see his energy slowing down once again.

July 26, 1995 / Fran's Birthday   Tim was sent home tonight by the nurses at the plant. He's running a fever, having diarrhea, nausea and, oh yeah, fatigue.

I thought of Elsa today. No one in group has heard from her in a long time. No one has been able to reach her by phone, and she doesn't return phone messages. I hope she is all right.

July 27, 1995   Tim stayed home from work sick. He has no energy and spent the entire day in bed. I took a vacation day from work to be with him.

July 28, 1995   We left this morning for Michigan. I drove till the other side of Ohio. Tim slept. He really shouldn't be making the trip but insisted on going. I told him that we could stay home because he is more important than this reunion, but he wanted to go. He wanted to drive to Flint, so he did.

July 29, 1995 / Family Reunion   It was so good to see everyone and meet new family members. It was also good to see Jalyon. We spent time with Tim's family too. Mom and Dad took us out to dinner. I spent time with Lee Lee, my closest cousin, which was well worth the trip. It was wonderful to talk with her and catch up on our lives. I told her about Tim and me being HIV-positive. It was something I had thought about a long time. I knew that I would see her at the reunion, and I was concerned about her reaction. She took the news well and tried to reassure me that a cure is coming soon. She had the usual comments and questions about how. We debated the issue of a cure until she realized that I'm the HIV-positive one and had a little more information about the subject than she did. Soon we were talking about other family issues. I am so glad she knows, but I made her promise not to tell any other family members, because my mother would come unglued. She understood because she knows my mother and our family. We talked about how each cousin, aunt, and uncle would take the news. We both agreed to skip the bull and keep it between us. Lee was glad I told her and said that she would be there for us when we needed her. She said that she'll be around even when we don't need her. That meant a lot to me.

August 1, 1995 / Return from Michigan   Tim spent much of the time lying down while we were in Michigan. Low energy and night sweats are a constant, nausea too. It used to be about once every month or so he'd feel bad, but now he has something that won't let him deny being sick. For a while, he used excuses like "I ate too fast" or "I'll get over it" or "I'll be all right tomorrow." He can't fool me. His skin has completely changed color, and he lies around for days at a time.

I feel helpless because I can't get him to go to the doctor or the hospital. His T cells are not improving, and I worry all the time. It's been a hard road watching him, being concerned about him and his treatment, yet watching my own health decline. He's not being honest with me about his health, but he hasn't been honest with me about his drinking either. Our medical understanding was supposed to be based on honesty. When questioned, he says that he refuses to worry me, so he continues to keep details of bouts with HIV from me.

The boys have been at camp for about a week and a half, and

we miss them a lot. Jalyon said, "I miss my brothers, but don't tell them." This house is so quiet. Tim is always resting, the boys are gone and Jalyon and I creep around here like mice.

August 2, 1995 / Ebola Thoughts   There have been outbreaks in Zaire of the Ebola virus, which, like HIV/AIDS, has a high mortality rate and is assumed by today's experts to have come from Africa. This scare has caused public health concerns in the United States. According to Dr. Don Francis, who is a twenty-five-year veteran of infectious diseases, Ebola and HIV/AIDS have little in common, and I agree. The fact that Ebola burns itself out quickly separates it from HIV/AIDS, which lives long in body tissues. People can recognize an infected person who has Ebola and take the necessary precautions to protect themselves. HIV/AIDS has the opposite effect. The public cannot recognize those who are infected during the long incubation period, so behaviors don't change. If millions of people died in a few months of HIV/AIDS, something more would have been done in the beginning to stop it, in my opinion. Unfortunately or fortunately, whichever way you choose to look at it, HIV/AIDS is silent for weeks, months and sometimes years, but it is still working hard to gain control within the body. The fact that it takes a long time to show up has slowed studies. Also, the fact that it came on the scene among gay persons was more reason to do nothing at first.

The main link between Ebola and HIV/AIDS is mortality. Ebola has a 70 to 90 percent mortality rate, whereas HIV, which causes AIDS, has a 90 percent mortality rate, which some with HIV/AIDS would debate. According to Dr. Francis, there are few viruses that kill so large a proportion of those who are infected. In my opinion, there is not much basis for comparison of the two viruses. America has feared such illnesses as polio, which kills one in a thousand people. When polio was found, it was researched until a vaccine was discovered to slow it and bring it under control. Also, it helped to have a president of the United States who was personally infected.

Changes that take place slowly, such as pollution, the ozone depletion and HIV, are growing dangerously out of control but are not going unnoticed by those of us who live each day searching for cures, reasons and answers.

It is my belief, because I am one, that women are forced to live in the realities of life because we so often become caregivers rather than care receivers.

8:50 P.M. I don't wish to tell only about what HIV/AIDS does to a body. On my mind tonight as I write is the need to use condoms when experimenting with sex partners. However, condoms are not a *cure*, nor do they protect 100 percent. Although I don't wish to convey a message of "have sex," I do wish, with all that is in me, for you to protect yourselves.

All children must know — living in the 1990s among fast cars, fast living, fast loving, fast money and bed hopping — that these behaviors are more deadly than ever. To talk about prevention, we adults must come clean about sex and the dangers that an active multi-sex-partnered life leads to. Adults today must talk about preventive measures, stressing abstinence.

Lines in the sand will have to be eliminated while many truths and life lessons are taught. The excuse of "do as I say, not as I do" is no longer something adults have a right to. Children are doing as we do, and children are having sex, using drugs and killing themselves and others. More reality!

Having a monogamous relationship is what we strive for, but unfortunately, monogamy is rare, and having unprotected sex with one person means having sex with each person that person has had sex with. The picture here gets pretty crowded, doesn't it? My message here is think first, but if you still decide in favor of sex, use a condom, use a condom.

August 3, 1995 I've come across a few disturbing facts since becoming a member of the Tennessee HIV Prevention Planning Group: African Americans represent 16 percent of the state of Tennessee's population and account for 35 percent of the state's reported AIDS cases and 61 percent of the state's reported HIV cases. Twenty-five percent of all persons with AIDS are between the ages of twenty and twenty-nine, which indicates that they were infected while teenagers. Teenagers represent 4 percent of the state's reported HIV cases, but 57 percent of those cases are women and black Americans. Less than half of reported HIV cases in the state of Tennessee indicate gay or bisexual risk behavior as the primary mode of transmission. These facts reflect Tennessee alone. Has the picture become clear yet? Do you see how large the scope of HIV/AIDS is in only one state? Do you understand? Do the math for the rest of America. If for any reason you do not, I will continue with national statistics. Hold on to your heart.

Seventy-seven percent of the 14,081 AIDS cases reported among women in 1994 were among women of color, even though women of color constitute only 21 percent of all women in the United States. This 77 percent figure is based on reported cases. The question is, how many unreported cases are there? And how high would these numbers reach if all women of color who are HIV-positive were willing to report their status? Consider that 75 percent of people with HIV/AIDS in the United States currently are homeless or in danger of homelessness because they are too sick to work or there aren't sufficient social services to accommodate them. Some services that are in existence are not trusted by women of color for historical reasons. Beaten down and made to feel second class to every other class of people lends reason to the 77 percent figure.

I went to an all-white Catholic elementary school in the 1960s, when it was popular to be black only to blacks. I live today with a scar in my hand because a white child was going to stab me in the face with a pencil. My brother saved my butt once again and kicked ass for his little sister, which was common for him. He had many fights because racism was everywhere and fighting in school was what we both did to survive. Over the years, I have had to release past negative experiences for the development of my own self-worth — not forgetting, empowering myself, is how I live today, educating tomorrow's generation about discrimination caused by race, gender and HIV/AIDS. But I will always, as will most women of color, remain on guard from the evils of discrimination that live within humankind.

At what price will we declare that our children have had enough?

Suburban housewives, inner-city teenage girls, middle-class yuppie women, actresses, models, IV drug users, college professors, upper-class women and corporate executive professional women have more in common than being HIV-positive. We global women of all colors hold the needs of our children, families, friends and missions in life close to us. HIV/AIDS-positive women have the same ordeals our HIV-negative sisters do. HIV/AIDS just compounds our problems. Through sisterhood, we will all remain strong. How often in my life have I heard about sisterhood, brotherhood and togetherness? We strive to unite but continue to fall short. With each decade, our society fails and we become wealthier, or do we?

August 4, 1995   Yesterday was a very emotional day for me. Tim stayed in bed and was unable to get up. He hasn't worked for the past three days, and when he does go to work, the company sends him home. He looked so bad when I walked into our bedroom and saw him lying still. I walked over to him, gave him a kiss, and he just lay there. The antibiotic the doctor gave him doesn't seem to be helping, but he is trying to wait a few more days before contacting the doctor's office again. I took one look at him and tears welled up in my eyes. Trying not to let him see me cry, I made an excuse to leave the room and went to call the doctor.

Finally I was able to get through to Bev, who told me that we have to give the medication time, and he should feel better soon. She said that he was treated for bronchitis, which explains the problem with his lungs, but she also said that he did not mention the blood in his urine, and he should come back and be checked for a possible urinary tract infection.

I spent time with Jalyon. She sees Mom crying and doesn't understand. My baby came to me and hugged me, and all I could do was cry. "Dad's sick, yeah, Mom?"

"Yes, baby, he is, and I am going to take care of him."

Aaron called from Atlanta to see how his dad is. Senior members of Camp Marymount went on a three-day trip to Stone Mountain, and the staff gave all the kids a chance to call home. Aaron was standing in line and couldn't talk long because the other kids were waiting to make their collect calls. I wasn't sure if he was having a good time or not. His conversation left me guessing. He is definitely ready to come home. I did get that much. "I'll come get you Aaron, when you get back in town."

"That's OK, Ma, I'll see you Sunday."

"Yes, son, we will see you and Brandon on Sunday for visitors' day."

I will get help when I need it. Be strong when
I can.
Lean on you when I lose faith in myself,
sometimes I lose faith too.
I will read. Learn. Listen. Love. Heal. Counsel.
Cry. Feel depressed. Scream. Hurt. Pray and
Heal again.
All in the midst of Family. Friends. Work.
Marriage. HIV/AIDS.
So when you see me coming you will already
know me when I get there!

After Sunday we will have one more week left, then home in time for Jalyon's birthday and getting ready to start school. I'll be happy to once again have my family around me.

August 6, 1995 / Sunday Visit   Brandon and Aaron came home for a few hours from camp. It was good to hear Brandon talk for hours about something that excited him. Camp is turning out to be a good experience for them. Aaron's having a few problems, but nothing that he can't handle. We washed clothes and bought junk food to take back to their entire cabin.

August 11, 1995   We will be together again tomorrow. I have missed my family. Yelling, screaming, fighting will soon fill the air in our house, but with three kids so close in age, it has become the norm.

The summer of 1995 has been one of separateness. First, Jalyon's going off to camp for a week, then a few weeks at Grandma's. Second, Brandon and Aaron going off to camp. Third, Tim being quite ill most of the summer. I have spent countless hours in worry over him. I am sustained only through faith. Through the stages of HIV/AIDS, I have become strong in my convictions and beliefs. Tim's alcoholic ups and downs affect us all. HIV-positive and convinced that he is facing AIDS, he has not stopped drinking. Two diseases face him.

August 13, 1995   Jalyon's birthday. She had tons of fun. Balloon fights in the den with friends were great.

August 15, 1995   Since the seizure that put me in the hospital, I have had two small ones, and recently I had another big one. I got that strange taste in my mouth, then I started shaking. When I came to, the bed was a wreck and I didn't recognize my own bedroom. I could not remember where I was. It was the middle of the night. Tim was on late shift, and I didn't wake the kids. I didn't want to tell anyone about it.

August 16, 1995   I found a good home for Thai. She has grown too big for our yard, so a woman at work who has a big fenced-in yard agreed to take her. We will miss her but can go see her any time.

August 20, 1995   School is in full swing, and it's cost us a quarter million dollars, or it seems it has. I pray that the children stay happy through the year.

Still haven't seen Elsa. I guess she can't make the two and a half hour drive in for group. I wonder if anyone else from group has heard from her?

I hooked up with Mark Jackson from United Methodist Communications. He's agreed to donate his time and talent to completing the video project. I think I have finally run across the person who will follow through. He has a laid-back and competent personality.

August 23, 1995   It seems to take special effort to get in front of this computer these days. I am at work full time and have been since July. Medical restrictions are still in force. I am also working very hard on the video, "Reasons to Live: Women, Their Families and HIV," which is moving wonderfully. These days, I interview people who want to participate as well as schedule the time, location and date of shoots. With word of the video spreading and the public's hearing about it, Tim and I have mixed feelings. There are so many things at stake. The ugliness of the stigma, job security, our sexuality, insurance and, most important, the children's safety and privacy. Tim and I discuss our concerns often, but we agree that this video and our willingness to move forward with our heads held high is our only choice. My direction in life is getting more people's awareness.

It's my turn. I am running a fever, glands swelling, sneezing, sinusitis ups and downs, you know, the usual stuff you read about HIV. While Tim *must* rest every day, I stay busy with school starting, working, the video, Cares' board meeting, state planning meetings, scheduling, running after this contact or that contact for the video, plus trying to have time for me. It ain't happenin'. After several attempts to contact Bev, I finally got through to her. She called me in a prescription for EES, which is the same medication she had Tim on all summer. The problem with me being on this medication is that it causes seizures, and Bev didn't tell me. Our neighborhood pharmacy caught the mistake. We are truly blessed to have friends who look after us.

August 25, 1995   Sitting still is not an option, because I am not sick enough to qualify for disability from the company and not well enough to work full time. Living in limbo each day is scary. HIV-positive women's lives are always, always in crisis, and I am no different. Fighting this ongoing cold thing is beginning to get me down, even with the advancement of the video. My concern has now shifted from Tim and his being sick with one thing after another most of the summer to myself. This cold has been dealing with me for two months. I feel defeated today.

For me, waiting to feel better need not be equated with waste. In waiting, I can learn patience and a different kind of control — self. Meditation can become a renewed preparation for whatever lies ahead for me and my babies. Illness and disability may become a time of negotiation with my higher power. I hope that negotiations in faith, as I wrestle with impending disability, will create growth in me.

Sincerity for me is found in the live radio show I was a special guest on last Wednesday night, August 23. Alicia Benjamin from the *Metropolitan Times* has been working with me and Mark Jackson on the video and asked me to be her guest on "Transformations," a live radio show at Fisk University. For an hour we talked about my life as an HIV-positive mother, wife and full-time employee. We even got callers who thanked me for my candidness and gave me words of encouragement. For the first time I was able to reach hundreds of listeners with the message of education and prevention. Trying to enlighten listeners, I told of how I found out about being positive and the virus's effects on my family. With carefully chosen words and no names used, I told listeners about my children handling the news and my most precious support system. I drove home the message for self-awareness and protection, women's and families' rights and the need to get information.

I hope I helped listeners understand life inside HIV/AIDS. Alicia was great with statistical information and contact telephone numbers for the CDC and Nashville Cares' Heartline. We spoke about the video, now titled "Reasons to Live: Women, Their Families and HIV." I asked listeners for minority participation but also let them know that stepping forward would mean possible national exposure. As I spoke to listeners, I forgot that I too have very much at stake.

August 26, 1995 / T Cells   From the very beginning of learning about this virus, I was told about T-cell counts. T cells are white blood cells that participate in a variety of cell-mediated immune reactions. Three fundamentally different types of T cells are recognized: helper, killer and suppressor. Each has many subdivisions. T lymphocytes are CD3+ and can be separated into the CD4+ T helper cells and the CD8+ cytotoxic suppressor cells. CD4 counts are a measurement of the immune system. They shows how the virus is progressing in the body and become more important as viral load increases. Some people pay close attention to T-cell counts, others believe that it is only a number and does not determine their general overall health. When the T-cell number is small, less than 200, the CDC considers it to signify full-blown AIDS, regardless of one's health, and some people have a problem with that. But others believe that this is the time to stop working, begin taking more precautions and manage health care more aggressively.

Opinions and attitudes change when watching the indicators of one's immune system decrease in number. The virus can control your body and life, as well as your mind. "It won't control me" has been said by the best of them, but it eventually does control your body and mind, therefore controlling your life. It is very difficult not to pay attention to changes occurring inside and outside your body and mind.

T-cell recognition does happen. The question most commonly asked by the women in my group and other HIV-positive people to other HIV-positive people is "What is your T-cell count?" Doctors measure T-cell levels to determine if and when a change in medication is needed. Blood drawing is a common occurrence during doctor visits. So you see, we really are controlled by T-cell levels whether we admit it or not. Monitoring one's health means monitoring T-cell levels. Choosing not to go to the doctor and get T-cell levels checked is only denial, because when the virus is present, it is constantly destroying T cells, which means that it is destroying the immune system. "Compromised immune system" is the term used most. The immune system comprises the lymphatic circulatory system, white blood cells and lymphoid organs and is an important aspect of the protective structure of the body. The circulatory system consists of blood vessels such as veins, arteries and capillaries. An entire parallel circulatory system known as the lymphatic system assists the immune system. This system circulates lymph fluid that surrounds the body's tissue. Lymph transports white cells, and lymph vessels drain lymph to lymph nodes. Lymph nodes, which are pea-sized structures scattered through the body, are found under each arm, under the chin, in the back of the neck, and in the groin area. White blood cells are the major active component of the immune system, and most doctors try to keep a close eye on the entire system.

I understand that T-cell news can be devastating. High, low, above or below 200, the magic number the CDC uses to define AIDS. Personally, I pay attention to Tim's counts more than my own, because his are lower than mine. He has taken AZT for over a year, but his T-cell levels continue to drop. It becomes depressing for him and scary for me, and those are the times when we understand why some don't want to know about T-cell levels. Damned if you do, damned if you don't. Controlling if you do, controlled if you don't. In some way, every day HIV/AIDS and T cells are controlling me. Even if choosing not to see a doctor becomes one's choice, wondering what one's levels are still hangs in the back of the mind.

While working on the video and interviewing HIV-positive women who have become close to me, I have helped one of them work through the crisis of an abusive HIV-positive husband. Another couple shares nothing except bills, child raising and denial that the virus lives among them.

Doctors usually tell those who are diagnosed, if they're starting off relatively healthy, "You have ten years, but we must monitor your T-cell count every few months." From beginning to end, we are slaves to our own immune systems. However, if we would take care of ourselves from the beginning of life, we might have a better chance of not becoming "uninsurable." I guess it is another thing that becomes common among us.

August 28, 1995   A friend is in the hospital for what amounts to depression, which caused her to relapse back to drug usage. Being addicted to drugs and being HIV-positive, plus her family's dysfunction, sets her up for bouts of depression. As we talked, I told her that the only difference between her and me is that she's in the treatment center and I need to be somewhere. I went on with these thoughts: My absence of light is caused by the situation at work and the unexplained fever that won't go away. At times the light grows dim and I search for wisdom from others to sustain me. In my climb of faith, I see through depression with my own wisdom, but why I yearn for others to validate my own self-worth escapes me. I know that it is not God's will for me to feel anxiety, depression and pain, and yet my mind is held to chains by darkness. I ask that this deficiency be lifted.

My prayer remains the same, to be brought home to truth, wisdom and a closer walk with my God. I am not sure why it seems so difficult to stay focused on the positiveness of life. Changing, growing, illness, looking for reaffirmation, encouraging souls in what sometimes is a lonesome journey become draining, and I do have weak times, as we all do.

When stillness and nonproductivity weigh upon me, like the weight so many Americans want to lose, that's part of the darkness I write about. People are only allowed to see the sadness that crosses my face, but the emptiness I will carry alone. I am quite thankful that the children fill up the spaces so the eardrum echo of loneliness surrounds seldom, but nevertheless surrounds. The inner peace I seek lies less in something new and more in my heart, where all that is me and important lives. Joan, my psychologist and friend, says to "punt" during these times.

Only love will bring happiness. Nothing else will complete me. To acknowledge love is to increase the capacity to heal. I cry. I know that faith is a growing process, one that must be worked on constantly. Don't drop the ball; fumbling is accepted. Finding my way when the light is seen only in shadows, I will give what faith I have willingly. HIV has come alive again, this time in the form of unexplained fevers, and that ever-present buddy of mine myelopathy just keeps hanging on.

August 29, 1995 / Crosses to Bear   When driving on the highway, look around you. The beauty is breathtaking. Someone close has an addiction to sleeping pills. The same person is also addicted to alcohol. These thoughts cloud my breathtaking view. A loving young mother of a two-year-old daughter is doubly addicted. Out of myself my compassion grows for her. Having nothing to offer but my own experience living with HIV, being a mother and being married to an HIV-positive alcoholic, I give.

A car now passes me on my breathtaking drive. A woman who appears long and lean wears a face brace. Careful not to look as her car passes mine, stone faced, looking straight ahead, she was unable to hide the uncomfortableness of her abnormality. I am moved to write about our personal cross because humanity, each one of us, will always carry some form of cross on our way to Calvary. Why? I don't know. But the journey to Calvary will be much easier when we work together and first realize we will have a cross to bear. Our family's HIV/AIDS cross has the potential to destroy life as we know it. Our family cocoon has been invaded, and without wonderful spirits surrounding us, our cross could become unbearable.

Picture Jesus on His walk to Calvary, where He knew what was at the end of the road. His stumbles and slips were comforted by the select few who chose to offer a helping hand. But along the way there were those who scorned, made fun, mocked and threw stones. Hearing this story as a child meant little to me. Today I take comfort in His journey because He will (through others) be with this family during the coming years of HIV/AIDS. I will comfort my children as the face brace gives support to the stranger. My breathtaking view will be restored.

I see the face of God in the mountains and His stableness in the ever-changing sky. Your cross may not be my cross, which is HIV/AIDS, but we each and every one will carry a cross. If today you have no cross, offer help to others, because one day when you least expect it, you too will have a cross to bear.

August 30, 1995 / The Year Within   They called it the "wrath of God." Many health care workers and even the average John Q. Public have referred to this virus as the "wrath of God" over the years. What kind of god do they know that could be held responsible for this illness? What god do they worship? Not the God I know.

I've seen a change in my medical support. Today, health care professionals are still learning about treatment, care and mental support for people with HIV/AIDS. Attitudes are changing from the early days of refusing to treat AIDS patients, and curiosity and questions seem to pour out. Nurses ask their patients questions about how it is to live with HIV/AIDS and how they can help comfort once-rejected patients. Can you imagine going to the hospital and being turned away because you are HIV-positive? Well, it happened, and it still happens today.

Almost a year ago, I met a slender, tall woman named Bobbi Lee at my women's group. She came stepping in with talk about nutrition and something called "healing touch." I listened to her respectfully but thought, "Yeah, right." I had to learn. We soon became friends, and she is a wonderful spiritual person in my life. She told me one day, "Catherine, you have inspired me to write a song. It is the first song I have written that is not a tearjerker or a 'woe-is-me.'" Feeling blessed and flattered that she felt so touched by me, I was honored to receive it as the music written for the video "Reasons to Live: Women, Their Families and HIV." Bobbi Lee wrote and sang "Untold Stories." You can hear it on the videotape. In it, Bobbi Lee sings of being one of "the chosen ones." To be a "chosen one" is not the result of the wrath of God, certainly not the God we pray to daily around the dinner table, not the higher power that has been present in my life since childhood.

The anger that lives within this virus is very real. Understanding that anger is as much a part of HIV as fatigue is, and that is sometimes forgotten. HIV seems to be a powerful magnet for feelings of shame, low self-worth and self-inflicted isolation. Withdrawal from others happens to most of us at some point in coping. Painfully inflamed emotions of anger have consumed me, and so many, many tears have flowed over this past year. Being unnerved by the sense of a virus lurking in the shadows has added an unpleasant element of suspense in my life. My feelings are often like those in this poem by Ian Mayo-Smith.

These feelings of despair,
They are not easy to shake off.
They will not willingly disperse
For they saturate the air.
I do not like the atmosphere
That they create about me now.
They make me dread the coming day
And fill me with an unknown fear.
Perhaps like morning mists
They can be made to disappear
When the sun shines really bright
Unless my spirit still resists.
This miasma of the mind,
It emanates from deep within,
So I must look within myself
If I am the source to find.
So help me through the coming day
To create a light within my mind,
A sun that shines and penetrates
And then the fog will clear away.

Ian Mayo-Smith

In our culture, women often feel insecure about their bodies and appearance, so looking good must mean feeling good — or so it is described. Not. Feeling bad inside happens to us all at times, but the problem with feeling bad about being HIV-positive is that I have nothing to focus my anger on. I can't see or touch the thing I am most angry at.

I will not speak for others, only myself, in saying that I was lost all my life, searching for something not quite found, not knowing what. Goal setting was never even thought about. Material wealth was the nearest thing to a goal I had. Choosing to be a part of the faces of HIV/AIDS was never on the agenda either, but it is my life now. I make no assumptions that our experience is exactly the same as that of other families who live with chronic illness. However, the emphasis is not on ready answers but on the struggles of this family to discover, for each day, the anger, empowerment, vitality and spirit within our home.

The distinction between sick and healthy can become confusing. It is depressing to think of myself as sick, but equally depressing to think of myself as healthy while having to worry about and make sacrifices to deal with medical issues for both Tim and me. HIV struck at the fabric of this family. All of us became disabled to some degree. If one member of a famly suffers, the entire family suffers together, and in many ways the family suffers separately as well. Pulled in so many different directions with the normalities of life, balance is shaken when disease decides to reappear and the direction changes again. This feeling is shared by most people with any chronic illness and in some ways has helped me during downtimes.

Living year to year with chronic illness changes your worldview dramatically. Normal routines and assumptions crumble under the weight of countless tests. Coping with the loss of control has been one of the most difficult adjustments we've had to make. Such surrender does not come easily, though. It means relinquishing my desire to plan ahead and to face the future with certainty. It goes against all my natural impulses. Tim and I had started planning for the children's futures long before HIV entered our family. Our retirement was plotted in advance as well. Individual retirement accounts and benefit plans allowed us to project comfortable retirement years long after the children were grown and out of the house. Like our parents before us, we had all those avenues planned carefully. When HIV showed up, it curbed my ability to plan ahead dramatically.

This year with HIV/AIDS has been a difficult year for us all. Only through faith have we come this far. The children have witnessed several changes, both liked and disliked, but nevertheless changes. As a result of my public work with education, we are likely to face change. As a result of exposure at the plant, we are likely to face change. Upon completion of the video, we are likely to face change. Through impending sickness, we are likely to face change. I had no idea that being one of the chosen ones could bring so much joy and yet so much pain.

September 1, 1995 AIDS walks happen in every major city in this country. Millions of dollars are donated and contributed for research, medication, food, housing and the basic needs of those who are touched by HIV/AIDS. The AIDS quilt travels the country, growing in both size and participants. Tears, so many drops of pain, witness the devastating effects of the virus.

September 11, 1995 / Jalyon's, Aaron's and Brandon's Birthdays
All the birthdays have passed, and we are still getting late gifts from Grandma up north. I think we all had good days filled with fun and gifts. Brandon's $100 went over well, and so did Aaron's CD player. Jalyon loved the party, and so did I.

I have been working on the video full force. Getting minorities to participate has been a challenge, and we are still looking. The women-in-prison angle has not happened yet, but I am not stopping. I really want them to be a part of this video.

The company has begun putting people out with restrictions. Some restrictions include lupus, numerous workplace injuries and HIV. This will include Tim and me. We go to work every day and wonder if we will be put out today. Difficult way to live. Very stressful.

Tim still tries to lie down during some part of the day. If he doesn't lie down I think he might fall down. We're still in counseling. That's good.

Women

Nature in motion with beautiful grace.
Comforting arms wrapped in years of tears.
Girls wanting to grow up fast but face the
    turmoil of womanhood.
Joys untold.
Leaders of mankind, empowered by self.
Minority, majority, entangled by oppression your
    mission becomes mine. Caregiving until it
    hurts, unmeasurable compassion.
Self-esteem is failing me.
Disgraced by disease, unable to make eye
    contact. Searching the winds through
    sisterhood to reach the plateau of timeless
    generations of womanhood.
All control is thin. Hold it. Fields of flowers we
    are not. It gets cold outside. Soft and cuddly
    hips to breast.
We are truly possessors of abuse. We are too
    many.
Listen as you hear the story of women.
Who I am.

September 14, 1995   Our marriage — well, our closeness is less than we both would like, but we are aware that our marriage needs work. Seems I have energy for everything except working on that lack of closeness. Tim does more to try to bring closeness than I do. I have deep-seated issues to deal with — namely, HIV and alcohol.

September 26, 1995   I am sitting in the cafeteria at the plant, where some of the restricted people sit who have no job. I listen to them tell one another the latest news about who was put out and why. It feels humiliating to sit on display surrounded by others with options. I think about what it's like to be here, and what other people living with HIV must be going through when their employers have no workplace policy to protect against HIV discrimination. It scares me. Leadership, both union and nonunion, has done nothing to place individuals with disabilities. Forcing disabled employees out appears to be the company's way of handling sickness, workplace injuries and terminal illnesses.

I pray I don't lose sight of the power within my peace. There is power in silence, and I will hold on to the silence and not give in to the company's apparent system of discarding restricted employees. I prepare myself daily as I walk toward the door and enter into what has been described as "being raped and having them stand over you laughing."

Tim has his own health issues these days. Bev wants him to start taking 3TC, but it's not available yet and won't be for about three or four more months. Not knowing if this medication will help his T cells elevate and stay up, he decided to wait rather than try to get 3TC through the underground method. Not much is known about 3TC, but what is known seems favorable. My understanding of this new drug is that after about six weeks T-cell counts rise and the virus decreases. I think about it a lot. Our lives together have changed so much this past year.

September 28, 1995 / Karen's Birthday   My reservations are made for the National Skills Building Conference in L.A.

October 1, 1995 / Group Troubles   Our family has been blessed lately. The kids are doing well in school, and report cards come out next week. I'm so glad for the blessing of my family's togetherness, because so many other things have distracted my thoughts.

An HIV-positive friend is in the hospital for depression, while Irene is dealing with another mysterious infection. They have no idea what it could be. The doctors wanted to operate and remove her appendix, but her temperature dropped dangerously low, so surgery was postponed. The women in group immediately went into action to help care for her daughter, Deondra, who has AIDS herself and is very sick. Irene's mother called asking for help with babysitting, so the group members arranged for her care. Irene stayed in ICU for four days and is now resting in a semiprivate room. She is still so sick, so weak and so much one of us. Her daughter stood wailing as the ambulance came again and took her mother away from the summer camp retreat they were at.

I got a call from another group member. She was crying and feeling very depressed. She had taken two handfuls of some medication. She tried to kill herself. I think it was more a cry for help, but who knows? At this point, my head was filled with what to do. She went over to Bobbi Lee's house, and I met them there. 911 was called before I got there, and she was taken to the hospital. My heart trembles for the women of WORTH.

Tim has never shown any interest in HIV/AIDS support groups. I wish he would. In fact, he sometimes resents my involvement with WORTH. I can't imagine going through HIV without any HIV friends to help. I think he would find it a great experience.

October 10, 1995   Elsa has died, and WORTH is heartbroken. The misery and reality of HIV/AIDS have taken one of us. I feel emptiness. How do I prepare to attend the funeral of a friend who has died of AIDS? How can I say good-bye to Elsa? Who took the owner's manual that tells me how to act?

October 17, 1995   I have waited a long time to attend the National Skills Building Conference, and now I am on my way to Los Angeles, California. I am lucky enough to be going on a scholarship from the National Association of People with AIDS and from the state of Tennessee. I enjoyed the in-flight movie.

I spent the day walking around the huge Century Plaza Hotel and outdoor mall. I bought T-shirts for the kids. The room is great, and so is the view.

October 18, 1995   Today was very encouraging for me. I stumbled upon two women looking for the National Minorities AIDS Council, so I decided to go with them. It turned out to be a meeting by and for women of color. These women want equality for women of color living with HIV/AIDS. I did not feel so alone. I became completely involved in everything that was said. I will work with this group to obtain equality for women of color.

October 19, 1995   The first part of the day I spent in the African American session, listening to people of color from around the country, including Hawaii and the Virgin Islands, talk about issues related to them, including the Million Man March that recently took place in Washington, D.C. Issues addressed were:

- blacks using the church as a forum to reach others in the community; the need to review and revamp HIV/AIDS education in black communities so all can understand the message and continue the message throughout life;
- the need to reach middle-aged, closed-minded minorities who think it won't happen to them;
- the need to reach minority women and get them to rethink sexual responsibilities;
- how to break the cycle of young minorities' beliefs and behaviors;
- needle exchange programs, which are working in metro cities;
- government accountability for narrowing the gap and being receptive to getting needle exchange programs implemented; and
- the effect on minorities if the 076 project (which is under experiment in New York) becomes law. The results are already bad, and 076 will impact women of color more than others, because minorities are becoming infected at a higher rate.

Women have been denied medical research for decades, but pregnant women have been denied more because of not knowing the dangers of medications to themselves and the unborn. Minorities historically have large families and will continue to get pregnant, and infected women will continue to have children because, culturally, that is what we know. Minorities accept the use of AZT at lower rates than whites due to medical gaps, lack of programs, lack of trust, and so on. Prenatal screening for HIV infection by risk will fail to detect as many as 70 percent of infected pregnant women because they won't go.

Minorities look to other minorities when it comes to medical issues and feel more comfortable with them. All cultures see the world through their own eyes of cultural experience. The O. J. Simpson trial was used as an example.

One good thing about the 076 study was that health care was better, while the study lasted, for those women than for poor women with no health care or limited access to health care.

HIV-positive women will continue to be sexually active.

In addition, it was submitted that the battle of 076 is already lost. Congress will make it law. We must come to terms with that and figure out where to go from here. The face of medical treatment is changing. Emotions will run high, and many people will choose to forgo medical treatment. Eliminating Medicaid is at hand — replaced with health care that will be affordable only to those that have. Sad.

The second part of the day I spent attending a session on women and HIV. I was charged by women of all races and cultures. I offered to chair a regional planning committee that will take a completed agenda to Congress. In my opinion, we must stop the infighting and come together for the whole face of AIDS, which includes everyone. Our lives are at stake. My life is at stake!

October 20, 1995   Today I woke up not feeling well. Myelopathy pain is intense. I went down to breakfast, and afterward I wandered around the display area and got a lot of information. From there I went back to my room, turned on the soaps and fell asleep. I felt fatigued, so sleep was the only thing I could do. Later, I forced myself to go to a session with Patsy Fleming, who represents President Clinton on HIV/AIDS issues in America. While there, I learned that the face of AIDS includes a single HIV-positive black man trying to raise his three small children alone, because his wife has already died of AIDS-related illness. He is sick and feels little support from the traditional groups. He said that he has yet to find a support group in his area for men living with HIV and raising small children alone. It touched me to listen to him. We can't forget any face. Then I went back to my room, ordered dinner and stayed.

Today I felt lonely. I guess it was mostly because I am not feeling well, but I just couldn't shake that feeling. The reason for my being here was all over me, and I wore the armor reluctantly.

Another lesson learned was the commonness of our concerns across the country. We are concerned about such things as medical expenses and long-term care, hospitalizations and doctors and whether we will be alone when we give up to AIDS.

October 21, 1995   I decided to spend the day at Venice Beach. Friends and I hired a van and took off. Venice Beach was wonderful. There are many shops, small restaurants and lots of people. Vendors are everywhere, and there is so much to spend money on. The walking around was great but very tiring. I did manage to stand straight all day. Collecting lots of shells was so much fun. Leaving the ones that we left was good too. I stood at the ocean's edge looking at a majestic vista. God. Tears welled up in my eyes as I prayed, remembering my reason for being in California. Also, thoughts of my family gave more reason for prayer. I cried a lot.

Later, after we got back, we parted. I caught two more sessions and then met my friends for dinner. It was the first time I could get dressed up, so I did. We ate at a Chinese restaurant not far from the hotel. After dinner, we went to the dance that the conference had scheduled. Several guest speakers, including Judith Light, brought a message of the innumerable men, women and children affected by HIV/AIDS. Each person who spoke touched my heart in a different way and that led to tears — tears of sadness, joy, pain and loss. There is so much loss. The reality of loss is the same as the invisible air we breathe. As one's lungs fill with air, HIV/AIDS grips someone. Kind, loving souls filled with words of hope and encouragement for people caring for people with AIDS. Hope for those living in the midst of AIDS and prayers for those we have lost.

October 22, 1995   Sunday. Last day of what is now the second HIV/AIDS conference I have attended this year. Like the first, this conference was very educational. However, I found this conference to be different in many ways. Much of the focus of this conference was on health care providers and agency workers, but I guess the conference was supposed to build skills. Don't get me wrong; all these people, agencies, skills and hard work are very important. However, I can look at HIV/AIDS only through HIV/AIDS eyes. Too many agency people were there and not enough people living with HIV/AIDS. How many HIV-positive people could not afford to come but really needed to be there?

Many front-line, caregiving fighters have so much experience and know firsthand the plight of living with HIV/AIDS. The skill of caring for HIV-positive individuals must continue to grow like the virus grows. These obviously big-hearted people are special. I just can't help but think that the more male and female HIV-positive people that can attend such events the better the final mission will be. Those living with the illness could learn the newest treatments. After all, we can bring a different agenda to the table for discussion. We have a different stake in the epidemic. We have our lives on the line. Agencies and their employees have budgets, money and jobs on the line. Are you going to work yourself or your agency out of a job? I hope so. This point was heard and expressed each day I was at the conference.

When HIV-positive people spoke at any session I attended, the floor was always hushed. The experiences they shared were invaluable — sharing days, hours, minutes, disease, deaths of spouses, deaths of children, lovers, illness experience, faith, divorce caused by the virus, hospitalization experiences, health care concerns, weight loss, pain, friends' deaths, family acceptance or lack of acceptance, food, drug experiences, trials, housing issues, daily fatigue, and so many more topics.

October 26, 1995   My writing has become more proactive. After coming back from California, I am aware of working toward identifying some of the more political issues. Congress's wanting to cut Medicaid is a political wrong. I have never been interested in getting involved in government. Until now. Government was not one of the things I wanted to get involved in. Until now.

Coming back from this conference, talking to friends and actually getting prayerful, I can only feel good about myself. I have written to Senator Fred Thompson, who is the Republican senator from Tennessee. I made a copy of that letter for my personal file. I will wait and see if he responds to my letter with a form letter written by a staff person. If so, I will know he didn't even read it.

October 27, 1995 / Why Alternative?   If you have ever gone to a chiropractor or had a massage or acupuncture, you have used what is called alternative medicine. People use the term alternative medicine interchangeably with many other terms. Alternative treatment refers to individual herbs or therapeutic treatments such as massage. Holistic approaches refer to systems of healing that incorporate the mind, body and spirit.

Alternative medicine has been around for a long time. Although its popularity has fluctuated considerably, alternative medicine has been around since the beginning of time. Each culture has its own history of alternative medications and treatments. Alternative treatment has grown in popularity since the emergence of AIDS.

Acupuncture involves painless insertion of extremely thin needles into the skin at specific points to help balance the body's flow of energy, referred to as *qi* (pronounced *chee*). When needles are inserted at the appropriate points, it is thought that energy is unblocked and a release takes place. Acupuncture is used to relieve some HIV-related symptoms such as neuropathy, fatigue and pain.

Dietary supplements are commonly used in an effort to boost the immune system. Garlic, Chinese melon and turmeric are used, as well as nonfood dietary supplements such as shark cartilage and blue-green algae, better known as spirulina. These supplements are widely used by those looking for good alternatives. Amino acids are used to heighten the immune system as well.

Traditional Chinese medicine emphasizes treatments that enhance the body in a natural way, thereby increasing the immune system's ability to build. Typical treatments may include drinking brewed herbs or teas, acupuncture, breathing exercises and massage of all or part of the body.

Body manipulation techniques that are used to treat HIV/AIDS include acupressure, Alexander technique, deep muscle therapy, polarity therapy, Reike, shiatsu, Rubenfeld synergy, Swedish massage and therapeutic massage.

Chiropractic medicine is a system of therapeutics that helps restore normal function by manipulation of body structures, especially those of the vertebral column. Chiropractors may be able to relieve joint stiffness and pain, which is another complaint of HIV/AIDS patients. Be careful when using a chiropractor, because some claims of relief are not true. Having worked for one in Michigan, I am experienced with claims.

African herbal medicine uses a variety of healing techniques, including spiritual and mystical practices and dance, along with herbal medicines.

Homeopathic medicines include minerals, vitamins and animal products given in very low doses. Homeopathy is highly individualized to fit each person's symptoms.

Ayurveda, the healing tradition used for thousands of years in India, is based on returning the body to a state of balance and health by emphasizing the body's natural healing abilities. Treatment may include herbal remedies, teas and medication. Yoga, nutrition and aroma and basic therapy, along with massage and detoxification through enemas or other cleansing practices, are used as well.

Psychoneuroimmunology (PNI) is a relatively new field. It focuses on the relationship of mind, body and spirit in fighting illness and maintaining good health.

HIV infection increases susceptibility to opportunistic infection and a more rapid disease progression. Nutritional intake is sometimes not adequate, and people with HIV may lose weight long before developing AIDS. One reason this happens is that throughout the progression of the virus, nutritional status is challenged by symptoms such as nausea, vomiting, malabsorption, diarrhea, oral or mouth problems and infections that impede fat storage. Nutritionists and dietitians work with people in designing diets that provide nutrients that may help bring some body mass back. Some practitioners work with mainstream medicine; others have unique approaches.

Some of these therapies have yielded positive results, and those who have been helped rave about their way of taking care of themselves. Most alternative medicine has not undergone the intense scrutiny and testing required by pharmaceutical drugs, so their safety and efficacy can't always be documented. In addition, some alternative treatments can be as toxic and as costly as standard medical treatments. And most insurance companies will not reimburse for alternative medicine.

The decision to use alternative medicine is a personal one. Becoming knowledgeable about treatment issues, both conventional and alternative, is important in itself. Talking to a doctor you have a good relationship with is strongly recommended. Vitamins and herbs are drugs too and should be taken as such.

Obstacles confront individuals who want to use alternative medicine — obstacles that limit progress in evaluating the benefits or dangers of such treatments. Some argue that significant research should be conducted in this area and should be funded by the government. Others argue that it is simply not possible to test all forms of alternative treatments presently used.

Visiting the library and getting reading materials will help with making wise choices about alternative medicines and treatments. It is a good idea to research both alternative and traditional treatments before going ahead with any form of treatment.

October 29, 1995 / Primary Care   Primary care doctors and HIV/AIDS doctors don't always keep track of who's monitoring what in patients. It's best to have one doctor with whom you have a good relationship. If you have more than one, take care to get all the information from each doctor and inform each of them of the others' findings, tests and results.

OB-GYNs have no idea how hormone replacement therapy will affect my HIV progression, and that concerns me very much. My breasts stay tender, and swollen nodes all over my body, especially in my groin, still occur. Sometimes node swelling causes me to limp. I will make an appointment soon to see Bev about a Pap smear and exam.

October 30, 1995 / Geriatric AIDS   An older man named Tom suddenly took ill. This sickness was quite different from his past illnesses. He had experienced arthritis, as so many people do, and

Grace is often Quiet
Providing a gentle touch, offering a prayer,
  wiping a brow or holding a hand.
We don't have to talk, just be present in the
  silence of grace.
Grace, a light living in our heart, given by God
  and expressed by our actions.
I search for more grace as I become still within.

had also been treated for minor heart problems, all attributed to his age and natural degenerative state. His doctors were well aware of his treatment and medications and had kept him quite healthy, until sudden weight loss, loss of appetite, warts and strange sores began to appear. Tom's family took him to the doctor several times as things began to change, but the doctor would only give him a different medication and send him home.

Rapidly, Tom's health failed. He had to be rushed to the hospital in the middle of the night because he was vomiting and sweating profusely. His family was alarmed that his heart might stop. Tom was admitted to the hospital, where several tests were run in an attempt to find out what was wrong. Finally an HIV antibody test was given as a last resort. Tom and his family were informed that Tom had full-blown AIDS, with a T-cell count of zero.

Confused and in disbelief, his family had to deal with the news of Grandpa's AIDS and the doctor's new medical plans. Tom had lived with his daughter, son-in-law, and teenage grandchild for almost eight years, so none of them understood how something like this was possible. They didn't know that Tom had been buying sex from hookers for companionship after his wife of many years had died and left him alone.

On the other side of the country, Tom's twenty-five-year-old grandson had been diagnosed HIV-positive almost six months earlier. Tony had not dealt with being positive until his first opportunistic infection. After getting out of the hospital, he decided to go home to Florida and tell his family. Tony had felt so isolated while he was hospitalized. The reality of his illness was more than he could handle alone. Tony was traveling to his family in Florida when he took sick again. After several days of laying up in a hotel room, he felt better and continued to Florida. When he got to his parents' house, Tony was told that Grandpa was in the hospital with AIDS.

While everyone was at the hospital visiting Tom, Tony told the family that he too was HIV-positive. Grandpa looked on with tears running slowly down his cheeks. Tony held his grandfather's hand. The family was overcome with intense emotion.

Geriatric AIDS is a subject not covered in the owner's manuals given out by doctors' offices and health officials. Yet geriatric AIDS is growing at an alarming rate. Older men frequent prostitutes and inject drugs too. Older women who find themselves with gentlemen callers welcome the attention. The loneliness of being without a spouse for many years draws older people together. Unprotected sex has always been the norm for their generation. Condoms were for their children and grandchildren so that they would not get pregnant. Most older people believe, and raised their children to believe, that STDs happen only to bad people or "ghetto trash."

Older persons learn about HIV through volunteers who visit nursing homes giving first-person accounts of HIV/AIDS. Older people living with families rarely associate themselves with such matters. When volunteers visit nursing homes, they find that most older patients tell them, "That's nice, sweetie, that you come to visit and tell us a story, but this has nothing to do with us." They don't say anything about the times Mr. Smith sneaks into Mrs. Jones's room in the middle of the night and makes his way back to his own room before anyone sees him, or when nursing staff, male and female, have sex with willing or unwilling patients. Geriatric rape happens.

Most of us now know that HIV/AIDS does not care about age, but the message is not clear to the elderly. Getting older Americans to understand and listen has proved very difficult. Alzheimer's disease and denial that the virus could affect their generation are two big reasons for the increase in geriatric HIV/AIDS. More and more elderly people are found to be HIV-positive or, after death, to have had AIDS. Coroners are seeing an increase in AIDS-related cancer deaths among older Americans. Families find it easier to deal with cancer than AIDS, but AIDS-related cancers are a fact among the elderly.

Signs and symptoms can be ignored, because many changes occur later in life. Menopause is always a good way to explain changes that occur in people. Men and women go through hormonal changes, decreased levels of activity, and appetite changes. There's nothing to worry about when doctors say, "It's just old age." Doctors are slow to test for HIV antibodies in older Americans. Treating mature patients with more medication as symptoms progress is today's norm for doctors.

11:30 P.M.   At the conference in Los Angeles, I met a woman about sixty-five years old, well put together and very intelligent. I saw her across the room and thought that she was a health care worker taking a class on treating women living with HIV/AIDS. During the class, we were asked to share issues that we found important or that would have an impact on others.

This woman stood and told how long it had taken before her doctor even considered doing an HIV antibody test. She said that it took six months, day-long tests, and decreased abilities before the Western Blot was given as a last resort to determine what was wrong. She said that she had been relieved to learn her results — not relieved to be positive, but relieved to finally know what was happening to her.

After months of learning about medication, good health techniques and nutrition, she was advised to seek a support group. She had heard of a women's group at a local church, so she went. When she asked at the church where the living with HIV/AIDS women's group was meeting, a man told her, "You must mean the sewing class that meets here at the same time."

"No," she told him, "I mean the living with HIV/AIDS women's group."

Like so many, she had contracted HIV from unprotected sex with an older man with whom she had had a brief relationship after her divorce.

She went on to say that she is currently trying to form an HIV-positive group for older people in her community, but so far, she has had little luck getting participation. Some older people who know that they are positive won't admit it. Going to a support group is a form of admitting to and accepting the virus. Others don't have a clue that they are positive, and still others are willing to die with the secret rather than shame family, themselves or close friends with such news.

Clinical trials for the elderly are almost impossible to organize. Most older people are taking medication for other illnesses and refuse to add to current medication. Because there is no information on the effects of experimental drugs on the elderly, many say a resounding "no" to the uncertain options that doctors and specialists offer. The few who are willing to participate and are in relatively good health must be monitored very closely. Problems with transportation, forgotten medications and loneliness make it difficult to conduct accurate studies.

Geriatric AIDS is on the rise. The numbers among women and minorities increase. Children are becoming sexually active at younger ages. And middle America still hides from the facts. We can no longer turn a blind eye or deaf ear to this epidemic, because everyone is at risk. We have no more excuses for our failure to act in the face of HIV/AIDS, and we can no longer blame differences in people or be deprived of courage. The future of all generations is at stake.

2:00 A.M. A mother's love is a gift most of us know. Mothers understand, always try to lend a helping hand and most often are there when the chips are down. Anything less is not a mother.

November 1, 1995 I am sick. Fatigue has me flat on my back in bed. Tim and I had planned a weekend in Gatlinburg, but we were unable to work out the details, and I didn't work on getting anyone to stay in the house with the kids. I have no energy but continue to force myself. Swollen hands and fingers have made it difficult to write. Node swelling has depressed me. Low-grade fever seems to strip away much-needed energy. I feel I can't be a mother sometimes. I can only sleep. Through sleepy eyes I wake only long enough to see the children as they come to check on me.

My mind wonders through thoughts of, Will I see them grow up? Will I experience grandparenthood? Or Will I see my sweet daughter graduate from high school? Will her dad?

I know why I fight within myself. I fight hard not to put on my HIV face for the world. I am afraid that if I stop the internal fight I will ultimately wear the face of AIDS. When first diagnosed HIV-positive, I reeled from anger — anger at HIV, anger at God, anger at the doctor who gave the test without my knowledge and anger at Tim for infecting me. The injustice of it all pissed me off. I tried not to let Tim see the anger and confusion I felt, but I knew that I was being unsuccessful in keeping those feelings covered. Continuing with that front for the world made me mad, and I resented trying to act something I wasn't really feeling. I still resent that. I also felt that AIDS was an embarrassment to me, to our home and to my marriage. Like a thief in broad daylight, some small virus was stealing my life from me. Questioning my sexuality, my husband's sexuality, his drug use, whether I had had blood transfusions with all the surgeries and doubting everything I held dear to me had me swimming, struggling to breathe, choking on *anger.*

I remember that for the first eight months after the surgery, I tried to maintain my dignity through the pain of a surgery that had not even begun to heal and the pain of invasion from a virus that only eight months earlier had meant nothing to me. But one long and lonely day it all became too much. I was a mental mess. I was desperate for answers, and my eyes were swollen over from crying. How can anyone surrender to dying? Why did I think HIV/AIDS couldn't come to my home? What made me think I was special, too special to get HIV/AIDS? I wanted someone to tell me why. I wanted doctors, surgeons and Tim to apologize to me for all the pain I felt. I wanted someone to take the blame for what was happening. I wanted to move past the anger and forgive someone, anyone for the pain — physical and emotional pain.

What I got instead was more pain. I could see in Tim's eyes so much pain. His body held so much sorrow, sadness, regret. He wanted to remove the curtain of pain from me and would have been willing to carry full blame, full responsibility for the illness that has manifested itself in our marriage. Tim would tell me, "It's my fault. I did this to us." Somehow, when he tried to take the blame it did nothing for me. It did not help for him to blame himself. After realizing this, it took a very long time to acknowledge that apologies coming from anyone could be given only if the virus had been given deliberately. Tim did not give this virus to me deliberately. HIV is here, which is a fact; it is also a fact that it was not deliberate. Tim and I would gladly wear the chains of HIV/AIDS alone to spare the other the physical and emotional pain we both have now.

Tim says that AIDS will be the cause of his death, but I think that drinking may be one up on him. His liver damage has been caused by drinking in excess. HIV, AZT, 3TC will progress his liver damage. It has become his ultimate challenge, a challenge that he cannot run from as he has run from so many other challenges in his life. Although he is an educated man and very intelligent, his habit of retreating from adversity has gotten him to this point. He can't retreat from the advancement of AIDS.

I wish we could go back to the dream we shared when Tim and I saw in each other a lifetime filled with fertile possibilities, when a house on the side of a mountain housed our love, when children would come to visit with grandchildren in tow.

November 5, 1995   I got a phone call from a woman I had never met. She said that she had heard about WORTH and needed a friend. I went to meet her. Sarah, a woman about twenty-three years old, shared with me how she had been diagnosed just after giving birth to an HIV-positive son. She wore his picture, which had been made into a button, on her chest. Her son had been born sick and remained sick throughout his short life. He had no idea what being healthy meant. He was on medication every day for recurring infections, fevers, vomiting and on and on. His mother was sick, depressed and helpless. She did the best she could for him. His father, HIV-negative, gave neverending support. He even lost his job because he chose to stay at the hospital with his sick son rather than go to work. Her husband's insensitive employer knew that his son was hospitalized with AIDS. A chill ran down my spine as she told me her story.

The young woman went on to tell me how she and her husband were systematically losing everything and that there was no money for food or bills. Their son was in and out of hospitals throughout the East Coast. Doctors were doing all they could, but the child responded to treatment for only short periods.

Their son died at age six of AIDS-related illness. As he lay in his mother's arms, she told him that she loved him and that he would be OK. The strength in her voice as she continued to talk gave the room a ray of hope that was short-lived. The ray died away after she stopped speaking.

My attention was drawn to the governmental issues surrounding AIDS and health care.

November 6, 1995 / Thankful   Channel 4 wants to do a complete story about the video. They read about the video in the *Nashville Scene* and wanted to talk to me about a story. I explained to them my concerns for my family and the publicity that could follow if I did this interview. I got peaceful and prayerful and searched for an answer.

10:00 P.M. Well, I have given it great thought, and I think it may be time for my work life and private mission to become one. I can no longer live in "if." It's time "if" got a life. My work with the video has taken me many places, and word has spread throughout Tennessee and the country.

The assistant warden at Tennessee Women's Prison has agreed to allow inmates to write me letters about their HIV status and treatment in prison. This milestone has been an act of God. I had called everyone, sent letters and still nothing. This accomplishment is God's hand at work in my life. I look forward to learning, growing as I hear from these women.

November 7, 1995 Tim is on sick leave. He got another cortisone shot in his elbow, but this time he was told that if this doesn't get it, he must have surgery. Along with the same problems he's had off and on for months, Tim's fatigue continues to depress him. Reassuring him that it's OK works for a while, but eventually the guilt comes again. Sick leave and his general body deterioration are hard for him to handle.

In the middle of things is news that a friend from work has gotten sick and died of AIDS. A young, black twenty-eight-year-old married woman went home to Detroit to die in her mother's arms. She left a long obituary telling how she felt about the virus. She had told no one at the company about her illness. This news has literally slapped Tim in the face. He had no idea that our friend had AIDS. Since he is not involved in any HIV support group, this is the first person that he actually knows who has died of AIDS. When I was told that she had had AIDS, I was not surprised; I had already guessed months ago. I kept silent and respected her right to privacy. I think of disclosure every day. I weigh the options. For almost two years, Tim and I have tried to bury our infection under the familiar warmth of our family. We tried desperately to save our family from heartless, cold people who might reject us and jeopardize our family's safety. There are so many reasons to fear disclosure — the company being a big one, insurance another. On any given day, one reason might take precedence over the other.

Photo: Brandon Jackson

Jalyon, Catherine, Brandon, and Aaron.

November 8, 1995 / Anniversary of My Father's Death   I thought the end of my life would be more sudden. I hoped for death to come quickly, like it did for my father. Rather, its gradual invasiveness whittles away functions and strength as slowly as the little old lady who drives two miles an hour in front of me. I still hold out hope for a sudden one. I'm tired of putting together a brave front, noble in adversity, the tireless soldier who projects all those qualities that are supposed to define terminal illness. I'm tired of saying "I'm fine" when in reality I feel like shit. Living is torturous at times, not only because of the physical pain of myelopathy, neuropathy and all those "opathies," but also because my husband is deteriorating before my very eyes. The torture comes unpredictably and whenever it wants.

November 13, 1995 / AIDS and Aaron   Last year, Brandon had classes on HIV/AIDS in Teen Living in middle school. At the time, he had just been told a few months earlier that both his parents were HIV-positive. I don't think he understood what he was being taught, but time has helped him get a better understanding.

Aaron is learning about AIDS at school, and it's hard on him. We talked about the other kids at school and their reactions to people with AIDS. He told me that the kids said things like:

- They should all be put in a line and shot.
- They should drop a nuclear bomb on all people with AIDS.
- All people with AIDS should just die.

As these comments were being shared with the whole class, my son sat at his desk filled with rage, not understanding how people could be so cruel. Aaron, they can be and are that cruel.

The teacher standing in front of a class may know algebra or English, but how can he teach HIV/AIDS with outdated materials and limited knowledge? This is part of the reason I do what I do. Through my work with HIV-related education, I dream of making a change in the information educators rely on. This is the future of America.

Aaron feels as though he has been slapped in the face again. The first slap was when I started having seizures; now the miseducation in his classroom and the hurtful comments of his classmates.

November 15, 1995 / "Mom, I Got a Cold"   During the first year after diagnosis, when I was learning about the do's and don'ts of healthy living, the kids got sick with one cold after another. Colds passed among them, just like the time Jalyon got chicken pox, then Aaron got pox, then Brandon got pox. With the usual concern, I tended to their runny noses, sneezing, fevers and plain awfulness. As I spoon-fed soup and hot chocolate, I often wondered if I would get their colds and infections.

What were their colds doing to me? Would I get pneumonia from my children, and would they feel responsible? Is that germ lurking in the air waiting for me to pass underneath so that it can find another warm host to grow and multiply in? If I sit on the same couch they were lying on, will some unwelcome germ be waiting for me? This is how I wrestled with my thoughts as I took care of them.

Sometimes my thinking would have me trying to keep my distance from my own sick child. Jalyon had strep throat and was very sick. I stayed home from work to nurse her back to health, envious of her immune system's ability to recover so quickly. I remember thinking, What kind of germs are they bringing home from school? They're kids, so they're not thinking about shared germs. They are at school with hundreds of kids and teachers who often don't think about the germs that pass among them.

As surely as the weather changes, the flu season comes. Jalyon was right on time again this year with strep. The doctor said that she had had strep at the same time last year as he wrote a prescription for a different antibiotic.

As with HIV, the flu has no cure. Different types of flu strains, from what I understand, make it impossible to find a medication or vaccination capable of eliminating the flu. However, some doctors and clinics recommend that most adults get the flu shot and pneumonia vaccinations every year.

The common cold has to be ridden out, sweated out, dealt with. I cannot run from the flu. I cannot run from a cold. Most of all, I will not be separated from my children because of the common cold or the flu.

As time has moved forward, and this family is well into the second winter season of colds and flus, I will not have my children feel that they have to quarantine themselves to protect me. Some precautions I no longer consider, because time with a sick child is precious time spent. Nothing less than giving myself to my children completely has ever worked for me, and I know that when they're sick they need me. As with all things, I will be with them through the cold and flu season.

November 17, 1995   An article appeared today in the *Metropolitan Times*. Alicia Benjamin wrote a wonderful piece about the video and my work with it. I sent copies to my mother and Nina.

Karen and I drove up to Fall Creek Falls for a women's retreat weekend. The drive was great and the company was good. The trees were rich with color, and the mountains showed me the face of God. The room Karen and I had overlooked a body of water with trees that grew out of the center. We spent Saturday morning sitting in lawn chairs watching the sun come up over the mountains, wrapped in blankets, temperature about forty-seven degrees, as we soaked up nature. We enjoyed herb tea as Karen read to me. I drifted in thought. This is a soothing, restful place to be. I felt my body become peaceful. It is a good place to retreat.

Outside my home, my friends Fran, LaVonna, Susan, Karen, Mark Jackson and Wesley Payne, all of whom are not HIV-positive, have given so much of themselves to me and therefore aid HIV/AIDS humanness. Lisa, Bobbi Lee, Irene, Roxanne, Deidre and all the women in my support group are great friends. Even though Elsa is not here anymore, I still consider her my friend.

Karen has become a very close friend who happens to be HIV-negative. She and I met almost a year ago at a conference in Kentucky. We lost touch after the conference, but she found my phone number and we have become close. She has shared her life and deepest thoughts with me, and for that I feel privileged. Karen's work with HIV/AIDS education at Meharry Hospital has given her a special insight into the plight of living with HIV/AIDS. She is thirty-three, is a vegetarian, attends dance classes, does yoga and takes piano lessons as well as several seminars to continue self-advancement.

One of Karen's special qualities is that she is a good listener. I bend her ear a lot, and she is eager to listen. She listens very carefully to my experience with the virus as well as all the personal stuff we talk about. I can tell that her brain is fast at work because of the way she says "Mmm" when I'm telling her something of great importance to me.

Karen and I spent a unique experience together this weekend. We allowed our lives to become quiet. We allowed spirituality, sisterhood, compassion, warmth and good music along with lots of nature to take us to that calm space known as serenity.

November 30, 1995 / AIDS Quilt at Tennessee State Museum Tim volunteered to work at the quilt exhibit. His job was to be quilt monitor. He took this responsibility very seriously. He said that he was honored to be a part of this event. Tim told me long ago that he wants me to make a panel after his death to be added to the quilt.

He had applied to be quilt monitor after I pointed out the application in a pack of mail I'd received. Susan came to see him. She stood with him and talked quietly. Susan told me that her brother, John Ford, had worked on the quilt and had never been the same.

Tim was on his way down to begin his monitoring duties but

came back upstairs to get me. "Catherine, I want you to come with me." I went with him.

It was the most powerful thing I had ever laid eyes on. Each panel represented a person who had died from the same disease I now have growing inside me — the same organism that lives in Tim. I walked, I stopped and stared, I walked up and leaned close to read each precious word. I touched, I held Tim's hand, I hung my head, I cried, engulfed in emotions, feeling the presence of each life now taken by HIV/AIDS. I am honored to be among you. Each vision I saw told a story. They told of lives lost to AIDS. They told of love. They told of people who were loved and who will be missed eternally. They told of families struck with the devastation of life lost to AIDS. They told of courage, of living with dignity with AIDS. They told of life!

The Names Project   The Names Project is a memorial to help bring an end to AIDS. It is a reminder of those who have died of AIDS. Its appearance helps raise money for people living with HIV/AIDS. This is how it started: A man named Mr. Jones painted the name of his best friend, Marvin Feldman, onto a piece of cloth. His friend Marvin had died of AIDS. Mr. Jones and some volunteers formed the Names Project in San Francisco, and people all over the country came to add panels for loved ones who had given in to AIDS. The quilt is now larger than twelve football fields.

The panels in the quilt are made by family and friends so that their loved ones who died of AIDS will be remembered. The quilt contains over 31,000 panels and is constantly being added to. Sections of the quilt travel across the country and around the world. As I walked from room to room, each experience catapulted me into another person's life. One said, "I love you, Mom." I fell apart. I heard my children saying, "I love you, Mom." I walked away from that panel with unexplainable feelings. My children will never, I pray, know how I felt.

I pray that God gives His gift of a *cure* to someone soon. One panel said, "When will man realize AIDS is real?"

Tim told me later, when we were on our way home, that he got through by telling himself that the room represented love and hope. "People do care, Catherine." Tim's leaving tomorrow for his first NA retreat. The group is meeting in Florida. This trip is very important to him. He went back to work last week. The doctor gave him several restrictions, and the talk of elbow surgery is now on hold because he needs to go back to work.

December 1, 1995 / An American Family   I've mentioned Ryan White before. He was a young boy who contracted HIV through a blood transfusion and eventually died of AIDS. Ryan and his family went through hell before his death. Ryan suffered more than an illness; he suffered the prejudice of having AIDS. His family's home was burned to the ground because Ryan had AIDS. His family was chased out of the home that Ryan lived in. His bedroom and everything dear to him and his family were destroyed. He and his family were treated cruelly by most in his community. Ryan was not allowed to go to school with the other children because Ryan had AIDS. No one should ever know this pain, especially a child.

What are the people in Ryan White's community thinking today? Are they remembering how sightless and heartless they were toward Ryan and his family? Do they dream about their souls? Do they regret their behavior? Do they still think that they were right? Most importantly, who in their families has HIV/-AIDS today? I bet they know lots of people with HIV. Some of them probably have HIV themselves. Finally, after Ryan died, a foundation was formed, and now that money helps others with HIV/AIDS.

December 2, 1995 / Alive   After viewing the quilt, I went into the recording studio so that the actress Wesley Payne could read my letters for the video. This was the first time someone had read them out loud — someone other than me. I've read several of them to my children, but no one else. Anyway, Wesley somehow made the letters three dimensional for me. They were outside me now. She read with conviction, breaking down as she read. She read letters I had written to my children. She brought to life the story of my life, the story of our lives. I cried silently. Watching Wesley through the recording studio glass, I relived my life. I relived learning that HIV had come. I relived those feelings she spoke of all over again.

I remembered. Wesley walked me through my life again. Wesley's voice will tell the story of HIV when the video is released.

The realization of HIV/AIDS came crowding in on me. The three-dimensional picture was me. I felt empowered, I felt humbled. I quivered within. I came home and played the copy Mark had made for me. Tim sat listening, remembering. When she finished reading, he held me. We remembered together. I played the tape again for the three children. They listened and remembered too. I am so grateful to Wesley for donating her time and talent. I could not have paid her what she's worth. Mark either.

Brandon has not been receptive to the letters I have written. I have not forced him to listen or read them, because that would be defeating the reason I write. But as Wesley read the letters, his face was still, his body not moving, engrossed in listening. Jalyon sat motionless; Aaron too. Quietly they sat and heard our family's story told by someone else. The next day, when I took the three of them to view the quilt, Brandon never left my side, moving to the next panel only when I moved.

December 4, 1995 During the dormancy of the virus in our lives, I have become a member of the Community Constituency Group. We are charged with interacting with the AIDS Clinical Trial Group.

The CCG provides fair and equal community representation in the scientific efforts, operations and activities of the ACTG. In doing so, the CCG provides advocacy, identifies issues, and presents possible solutions to the HIV research efforts within the ACTG. The CCG watches the protocol activities of pharmaceutical companies, which sometimes have their own reasons for not doing what is expected of them — *money*.

3:00 P.M. I've been in Washington, D.C., for twenty-four hours and have been in several meetings surrounding pediatric and adult HIV/AIDS clinical trials and research. Some terms that ring out constantly are:

- recompetition
- protocols
- powers that be
- co-chairs

- amends
- grant writing
- funding
- principal investigators (PIs)
- research
- carve-out money
- bidding for same dollars
- scientific agenda
- pediatric executive committee
- combination therapy
- end-point relative hazard

Oh, the bureaucracy, the weight, the heaviness go far beyond anything representing human. Learning acronyms for all the agencies won't be easy. I try to understand the reasoning for all this.

Affected and infected individuals expressing opinions and statistics still sing in my head. I can surely tell those people who are affected/infected from those who are not. A mother of two adopted children with the virus sits on the edge of her seat expressing her concerns about pediatric injustice. Infected people hurl their disdain toward those who make decisions for them. I bring the same agenda to the CCG table that I bring to the Tennessee State Planning Group table. I sit in these meetings listening and listening to one person after another. I hang my head in disgust. My heart is worn with bureaucratic overload.

People, companies and the stock markets are making money from AIDS. People are making big money from those who are suffering, living, trying to find some dignity in dying from HIV/AIDS.

The virus hasn't changed much in all these years, and the outcome remains pretty much the same — read the history of HIV/AIDS. Much history has focused on research and protocols, but that's about all. What about lives already lost? New medications have been added to the already innumerable marketed medications, including 3TC.

The good-old-boy way of handling the medical community is the way business has been run for years. They control the major committees; they run the most important trials; they determine what gets published and who gets promoted. It's been that way since the very beginning of structures like the National Institutes of Health and the Food and Drug Administration.

Thank God for the gay activists and ACT-UP front-liners who brought us this far in what they saw back then as a fight with the government. Gay white males and ACT-UP have provided direction through their strong efforts to make themselves known to the government, by storming offices and having their say in congressional hearings. No other disease known to humankind, including cancer and heart disease, has ever achieved such a demand for change. The government was challenged for the first time and didn't like groups of gays telling it anything. Some resentments were strong.

December 5, 1995   In 1995–96, the fight continues. Now we, the new HIV/AIDS generation, know and learn from them. We carry history, our history, and more — more educated and truly aware that, yes, we are still here.

As the virus inside me grows, more people with HIV/AIDS have joined the fight, and now we stand together as all the faces of AIDS to ensure change. I know, as we all do, that strength is found in numbers. Many voices make more noise than one.

We are not alone in the journey. The unshakable presence of Jesus is with us. I feel that this virus, this evilness, this viral visitation, is from hell. It is not from goodness, it is not from the Light. I am not worthy to judge someone's lifestyle, nor do I think that another human being is worthy of passing judgment, even though some think they are. No human being is deserving of this curse, regardless. I don't understand the whys of HIV/AIDS, but knowing that it is not from my Higher Power, a protector and immediate presence, brings me peace. Though I know that HIV/AIDS will someday overcome me, I will never quit trying to help others in whatever way possible, never stop trying to become closer to God and stay in His presence.

December 7, 1995   I would like to be a long-term survivor of this virus, but I can only hope and pray. Living with HIV/AIDS has a way of forcing one to look differently at one's behavior. A few common characteristics for living longer with HIV/AIDS include:

- a sense of influence or partnership in one's own health care
- a sense of personal responsibility for one's health
- a sense of purpose in life and one's ability to find new meaning as a result of diagnosis
- personalized coping skills that one believes to be beneficial to good health
- a physical fitness regimen, which may be as simple as walking or some other form of exercise
- dietary and nutritional changes
- an exchange of information with a supportive contact person with the same diagnosis
- open communication about one's concerns
- healthy involvement with other infected and affected persons
- the ability to withdraw from overtaxing involvement; nurturing oneself
- the ability to say no
- acceptance of the reality of the diagnosis without perceiving it as a death sentence
- a sense of unfinished business, goal setting, that more life experiences await
- discovery of a new spiritual level, unknown before diagnosis
- greater sensitivity to one's body and mind

December 10, 1995

My Dearest Brandon,

Sadly and often, much too often, in science there are career-making diseases. HIV/AIDS unfortunately happens to be one of them. As the numbers rise and we know people that have died of AIDS, and my friends begin to die of AIDS and people that they know die of AIDS, as the numbers increase, I feel burdened — hopeful, but burdened.

I talked to Roxanne today. She was not in good spirits this time. She did not speak of a *cure*, because she knows that it's too late for her, but she spoke of meeting her spiritual quest. She talked about going to the candlelight vigil at Legislative Plaza and what that meant to her. While there, she learned that over four million people have already died. She said, "God knows how many are infected." We are not always spiritual; we do not always feel blessed; we are not always up; we do not always feel like fighting.

"Catherine," she said, "giving my sons to my sister was the hardest thing I have done." Rox told me, "You can't imagine how hard it was to stop being a mother. I know it was the right thing to do, and I know my sister has been and will be a good mother to my boys, but you can't imagine how hard it is to not be a mother after all these years." She gets call after call from funeral homes wanting to sell her a funeral. I can't comprehend not being a mother, after all the years of mothering; to have to give up my children because I know that I have no choice. I only pray I will never be faced with Roxanne's decision.

December 11, 1995   Went to Dr. Woolridge, who put me on sick leave.

December 12, 1995   The decline in Tim's T-cell count while taking AZT has meant the introduction of combination therapy, AZT/3TC. The toxicity of AZT has haunted me since the first pill was taken. Now another drug with a short, unknown history brings me to new heights of uncertainty. Tim and I are reading clinical trial studies using AZT/3TC. I am able to get information from the ACTG and CCG.

3TC is made by a large pharmaceutical company that has a history of moneymaking. Studies conducted by it show that 3TC produces the best results when taken with AZT. Its results show an increase in CD4 counts and a decrease in viral load (the amount of virus present in the blood). Doctors who need this information to help with treatment planning are finding it difficult to obtain viral load testing for patients with state health insurance. At present, state insurances want more information about why viral load testing is so important. The cost of viral load testing is in question.

Anyway, these studies, thus far, are very young. Research has been short — eight months to one year. What happens after that? What are the long-term residual effects on the body while using AZT/3TC? I pay thoughtful attention to Tim, AZT/3TC and HIV/AIDS.

December 20, 1995

Taking care of me
Tomorrow's awareness haunts me
Living in the moment is where I strive to stay.

December 30, 1995 / Our Anniversary   I move toward the upcoming year reluctantly, cautiously. I cannot help the foreboding feeling I have for the events of 1996. I know that I must bring the year in with prayer, asking for strength and wisdom, asking God to go with me, because this feeling, as much as I want it to, won't leave. Looking forward to the release of the video in February and the four trips I will take during the year with the CCG doesn't do much for me now. My thoughts are about the sickness that awaits, about the loss that will come. I am not ready for that. I am not prepared for more loss, sickness or AIDS. I will never be ready for AIDS. How does one prepare oneself for AIDS loss?

The urgency to move toward faith is stronger than moving toward the new year. The positive things that I know will occur throughout the year take a backseat to the pain that my heart will surely feel.

I am grateful for the growth I have experienced during 1995. The grace of God has allowed me to love much more; it has given me a wonderful network of friends who care for me and my family. However, pain and hurt are all around me. It comes in the form of my heart being ripped apart by savage, brutal acts of HIV/AIDS, none of which is small to me. ∎

▪ Some Questions to Ask Yourself ▪

BECAUSE YOU HAVE TAKEN THE TIME TO READ THIS book up to this point, I feel that it is important that you, the reader, ask yourself a few questions. This questionnaire was placed in the middle of this book because each one of us must become personally involved. You have read thus far about a mother who was diagnosed as HIV-positive. The shock of the diagnosis almost destroyed me. Please take time to think about and answer these questions. They could save, or at least change, your life. A person who has AIDS may look and feel perfectly fine. The only way to know for sure whether or not you are infected is to get tested.

1. Have you shot drugs or shared needles with anyone?

2. Did you have a blood transfusion between 1978 and 1985, or have you ever had one abroad?

3. Are you sexually active or thinking about becoming sexually active?

4. Do you know if your sexual partner is HIV-negative?

5. Do you know exactly what your sexual partner does when he or she is not with you?

6. Do you know your sexual partner's past drug history?

7. Has your sexual partner ever had sex with anyone who has shot drugs?

8. Do you or your sexual partner work in a job where you might get stuck with used needles or splashed with blood?

9. Do you think you have any high-risk behaviors?

11. Do you think any of your past or present sexual partners have had high-risk behaviors?

12. Have you ever had anal, oral or vaginal unprotected sex (i.e., without a condom)?

Questions 12–16 are for women.

12. Have you asked your sexual partner to wear a condom?

13. Has he refused to wear a condom?

14. Have you had an abnormal Pap smear, prolonged bleeding, premature menopause or other frequent female problems?

15. Are you pregnant, and do you have any reason to be concerned about your baby?

16. Do you think that using the pill, diaphragm, foams, Vaseline, baby oil, body lotions, or an IUD will protect you from becoming infected?

The remaining questions are for both men and women.

17. Have you had same-sex sexual intercourse?

18. Has your partner had same-sex sexual intercourse?

19. Do you have any reason to be concerned about HIV/AIDS?

20. Can you tell by looking if a person is HIV-positive?

21. Are you infected and having unprotected sex?

22. Are you knowingly having unprotected sex with someone who is infected?

23. Are you HIV-positive and feel that you have no one to talk to?

24. Are you experiencing unexplained or unwanted weight loss?

25. Is there any history of sexually transmitted diseases in your present or past relationships?

Have you been tested? If you answered yes to any of these questions and have not been tested, it's time to consider a test. Health departments, clinics and doctors' offices are safe places for obtaining an HIV test. Call your local health department or your primary care physician for assistance. There are many resources available. Whichever you choose, make a move to be tested.

You should know that if you answered yes to question 21, you are committing a felony. If you answered yes to question 23, contact your local health department to find out about support groups in your area. ▪

1996

The long walk in the dark

I see no light at the tunnel's end,
So bring your flashlight with you, friend.

Shine your flashlight all around,
Check out the walls, check out the ground,
Check out the ceiling above your head
And don't let your batteries run dead.

Check out the path one step at a time.
Does it run level or is there a climb?
Or maybe it goes down in a dip?
Is the surface wet? Take care you don't slip.

There are rocks on the path. You may stub your toe,
So be very careful the way you go,
But don't give up, keep moving along
And to keep your spirits up whistle a song.

It helps if you move with a group of friends.
The light of your combined flashlights blends
And illumines the tunnel, makes the path clearer
And seems to bring the end of the tunnel nearer.
If you get depressed, shine your light on the walls
And read the graffiti there which recalls

The others that passed this way before
Whose courage took them to Nirvana's door.

For at the end of the tunnel we will see light.
It's the light of truth and it's blinding bright
And we shall see we're healthy and whole
After the long dark night of the soul.

Ian Mayo-Smith
June 20, 1996

January 1, 1996 / New Year's Day   Celebration took the old year out. Tim and I wanted to spend this New Year's Eve with the family, so we watched the time tick in the New Year and drank sparkling nonalcoholic grape cider in celebration. It was a time for toasting the future with firecrackers that filled the densely foggy night air. The kids and Tim rang out with laughter. I sat by the warm fire reflecting on the past year's growth prayerfully, my heart filled with love, hope, my mind filled with dread for what will face us. After the midnight hour had come in and the noisemakers had quieted, I went upstairs to hit my knees in prayer, prayer for protection in the long year ahead.

Tim asked me to make a doctor's appointment for him tomorrow.

January 3, 1996   Tim went to 3Cs today with the same problem he had last month. He has difficulty breathing, and he coughs a lot. When he first began having problems with his lungs, they seemed to bother him mostly in the morning. He would wake every morning complaining of his lungs hurting and a tightness in his chest. He would cough until he would bring up hard, brown masses of junk. That was how it was at first. Now his chest is always tight, and he coughs all the time. It's a dry, hacking, constant cough that hurts because it happens so much. Last month, Bev gave him a standard antibiotic as usual, and he took it as usual. Now he's right back with the same lung complaint. He told me that his lungs started bothering him before he went to the men's retreat in Florida and the problem has not improved but has in fact gotten worse with time.

At today's appointment, he learned that his T-cell count is down to 273. HIV is closing in, and the government's definition of AIDS is only seventy-three small T cells away. The doctor told him not to be concerned about the decline in the numbers, but he is

135

concerned, as am I. They told him to give the 3TC another month and then come back in for lab tests again. They said the numbers should improve, "Don't worry." It all seems contradictory to me. As HIV continues to multiply and the T-cell numbers decline, we are told not to be concerned, but Tim has to report each month to have his blood drawn so the doctors can monitor his levels. But we are not to concern ourselves with numbers!

I think the doctors and nurses don't know what to say to patients except "Don't worry." I think they prescribe medicine in the dark and hope for the best. What doctor or treatment has saved the life of a person with HIV/AIDS? Ultimately, life is only prolonged. Combination therapy, as it is now called, prolongs life, prolongs HIV, but it doesn't save anyone from dying of AIDS. *I hate HIV/AIDS.*

Policies about whether or not to take flu shots have changed at the AIDS clinic. Last year, they insisted that every patient get one. This year, they recommend that patients not take the shot. What are we, the patients, supposed to think when the medical professionals don't know what to recommend? Doctors, nurses, patients, researchers are shooting in the dark after entering the second decade of AIDS. We still have no clue, no cure. We still have AIDS. The confusion in the medical establishment should be of concern to everyone, whether infected or not.

I see this family's future growing smaller with each missing T cell. The children's questions have become regular now. "How's Dad?" "What is your T-cell count, Mom; what's Dad's?" "What does that mean? Is Dad going to die?" "He's sick a lot because of AIDS? Are you all right, Mom?" "Can I help, Mom?" Comments like "Mom, I don't want Dad to die," "Mama, don't die and leave me," are parts of our conversations now. I've also heard them say, "I hate AIDS." Sometimes I am caught off guard by their comments and left speechless by their ability to grasp the events AIDS brings. I have educated myself and others over the past year as I knew I would, but I have begun to realize how much I have educated my children as well. They are definitely paying attention.

My heart is still heavy and filled with dread as I continue to smile, make dinner and go about everyday activities. My husband's health fills my life's plate, and there isn't much room for my medical concerns, even though my own health is in steady decline. I can't stand to look at any tomorrows, because the numbers that mean nothing seem to get smaller with each one. AIDS has proved to be bigger than any man, woman, child, medication or government of this world. As we come closer to AIDS, I tremble with fear. I feel numb again — numb like the aloneness it is to face a diagnosis of AIDS. Hundreds of thousands of people have been diagnosed with HIV/AIDS. Millions have died of AIDS. There isn't anything anyone can say to help me feel better, no words of comfort. That strength is found within. If togetherness could change AIDS, many families would not have already gone through what this family is facing.

January 6, 1996 In 1996 I will remain steadfast in prayer and meditation. For my friends I will give thanks; for my family I will remain humbled; for the people of the world that are homeless, hungry, sick, rich with material wealth, I will ask God's blessing.

January 9, 1996 / Technical HIV/AIDS Information Recent studies demonstrate that T-cell depletion and disease progression are associated with increased viral load in the blood and suggest that the cytopathic effects of viral replication or the immune response to expressed viral proteins is a primary contributor to the progressive deterioration of immune function following HIV infection.

What this is saying is that the population of HIV in a person begins to outgrow the immune system's response to medications given. Therefore, as HIV progresses, the body becomes weaker, and more medications are introduced in combination to try to help the immune response. It is important that viral load tests be given.

Antiretroviral drugs include reverse transcriptase inhibitors, nucleoside analogs, AZT (sometimes called ZDV), ddI, ddC, d4T, 3TC, non-nucleoside analogs, nevirapine and delavirdine. Each nucleoside reverse transcriptase inhibitor has its own unique properties in terms of activity, tolerability and resistance. Strategies for anti-HIV therapy must include consideration of when to start therapy, what therapy to initiate, how to monitor therapy and what to use as second and third therapies when the current therapy begins to fail. Some people may not benefit from anti-HIV therapy, particularly those with advanced HIV suppression and prolonged prior use of HIV therapies such as AZT. Until recently, all the FDA-approved agents were reverse transcriptase inhibitors. Saquinavir, a new medication, is the first protease inhibitor to be approved by the Food and Drug Administration. Other new medications on the market include indinavir, ritonavir, AG-1343, VX-478 and U-103017.

The clinical efficacy of the protease inhibitors has been measured with surrogate immunologic and virologic markers, CD4 cell counts, p24 antigen levels, and viral RNA concentrations. The effect of protease inhibitors on survival and the clinical progression of HIV infection is unknown, but the opportunity to combine two agents with different sites of action in combating HIV infection is the direction in which medicine is going, even though that direction is unclear. HIV is not only a challenge to the person infected but also a worthy opponent to the medications being invented to control the spread of HIV in the body. The medication becomes confused after prolonged usage, just like inventors become confused.

January 11, 1996 / United States Military   It has become apparent to the leaders of this country that HIV/AIDS has also enlisted in the military. Many men and women are being thrown out of the military because ignorance still runs wild on Capitol Hill.

Legislation has been under construction in the Department of Defense since May 1995 that will expel all military personnel known to be HIV-positive or known to have AIDS. So far, the news media have downplayed this subject, and it is not well known by the public. Upon entering the military, an individual is given a battery of tests to see how healthy he or she is. Different shots are given to protect personnel from viruses that are found in this and other countries. Blood is drawn to determine if any viruses already exist. The bill presented by Senator Bob Dornan, a Republican from California, will likely pass the Senate this year, and those known to be infected will lose benefits, rank and education. This is not the first bill of this kind proposed by Dornan. At one point, he offered an amendment that would discharge all people with disabilities from the military. I wonder what his disability is?

Photo: Ian Mayo-Smith

"They're going to publish my book!" The family celebrates with Dr. and Mrs. Lemon.

Large HIV/AIDS organizations monitor legislation as it makes its way through the legislative process. So do I. Thus far, it seems politically correct to throw out HIV/AIDS-infected people who hold military jobs. How can the same government protect the rights of the same people it regards as useless? How can the government be held accountable for ensuring fair treatment in cases of discrimination by other employers when it tosses aside those who have volunteered to protect this country? I know not the fate of this country.

January 12, 1996   There have been many firsts since Tim and I were diagnosed:

- first time Tim took AZT
- first time I sat in the leather-covered chair I was sitting in when Dr. Richard delivered the news that changed my life's direction and my family's future
- first time I met a women of color, Deidre, who shares the same concerns, the same virus, the same uncertainty, confusion
- first time Tim started taking 3TC

- first time I went to an HIV/AIDS clinic
- first time I met another person, Lisa, who was HIV-positive
- first time I met a child, Deondra, who has AIDS
- first time I read about HIV/AIDS
- first time I told anyone I was HIV-positive
- first time I visited a friend with AIDS in the hospital
- first time I saw a ward in a hospital filled with people with AIDS
- first time I was blown away by the devastating effects of HIV/AIDS
- first time someone I knew died of AIDS
- first time I mourned an AIDS death
- first time I went to Nashville Cares
- first time I came face-to-face with the prejudice and stigma of HIV/AIDS, and that stigma was placed upon me
- first time HIV/AIDS entered into a conversation with my children
- first time my heart felt the burden of being HIV-positive
- first time isolation from diagnosis came upon me
- first time I questioned myself, faith, God, and all that I hold dear
- first time I did not think anyone would survive AIDS
- first time I saw the quilt

Unfortunately, there will be many more firsts for me.

No one with HIV/AIDS can forget the hour, the place at which the news was delivered. We may start off in denial, but we don't forget. I won't forget the exact moment my world became different, changed forever because I was transfixed with HIV and HIV began to transform me. I think about why I have "it."

January 15, 1996 That divine truth I search for seems to get lost under daily obligations along with the rhythms of our lives. Truth keeps getting buried under problems of alcohol that have carved a space in my marriage and my children's lives as well. Alcohol has been suppressed but has not left.

HIV, the bigger picture, stands before me, wrapped in the vows of my marriage. Tim's four NA meetings, on average, a week, lengthy conversations with sponsors and close friends in recovery, the twelve-step program, social gatherings, picnics, belly button birthday parties, mentors with years of experience and words of wisdom, retreat weekends, Deepak Chopra's book, *The Seven Spiritual Laws of Success,* marriage counseling, special counseling sessions, phone numbers exchanged with support people, HIV/AIDS, Retrovir (AZT), 3TC, days of not being able to get out of bed, nausea, vomiting, blood in urine, headaches, chest pain, skin rashes, skin discoloration, opinions of others, neuropathy, fatigue, stomach pain, throat pain, doctor's advice, prayer, knowing the error of his ways, nothing has changed the ever-presence of alcohol in our marriage.

My husband is no longer in denial about HIV/AIDS; in fact, he has educated himself very well on the total picture of AIDS. He knows all about the medications he takes. He reads every book, article and newsletter that comes into this house. He therefore knows what he's doing. His choice is his choice. He knows that the choice of alcohol is the wrong choice every time he chooses to drink, every time his sponsor confronts him, every time I look at him, every time he drives to a store to spend money on alcohol, every time he denies that he has been drinking, every time he admits to drinking, every time he feels sorry for himself, angry at himself, disgusted with himself. The cross of alcoholism has been carried a long time.

The effects shake my soul as I watch my husband's personal mission — shortening his life with alcohol before AIDS makes him someone unacceptable to himself. Alcohol has been part of his life since the age of fourteen. For over twenty-four years, alcohol has woven its way into the fibers of his blood like HIV. Nothing seems able to stop his mission of self-destruction.

My husband still drinks.

January 19, 1996 / Forced Disclosure and Other Issues The time has come for disclosure, "going public." The phone rang at about 2:00 in the afternoon; it was my only friend at the plant. "Catherine," LaVonna said, "your secret is out, and has been for a while. I didn't want to tell you, but you need to hear it from me before you hear it from someone else. Everyone knows you have

AIDS. Those letters you were concerned about have been copied, and those copies have been distributed among people on the floor." My heart stopped as her words rang loudly in my ear.

Living in fear is an uncomfortable existence, but that is how I have lived for almost two years. The secret of my health was, I thought, well guarded from fellow employees. I learned that it is no longer a secret. Assemblers at the plant know, or think they know. The word is, "She has AIDS." The fact is, I am HIV-positive.

When my good friend told me, I became shaky and began to cry. It all rang so true to me as she unfolded the story. Now I see why I haven't gotten a job or been placed on a work team all this time. The discrimination I have lived with since the letters were first lost all seems to make sense to me now. For some reason, I thought that I could protect myself from the living evil, but I was naive. I cannot protect anyone from the discrimination to which we are subject. This level of HIV has been very much an eye-opening experience.

January 21, 1996   Mark and I are working against a deadline getting the video ready to submit to two film festivals. Getting it completed has taken almost a year, but it has been an experience bursting with growth, hope and promise. My heart leaps with anticipation of a completed video.

The hours of video viewing, interviews, travel and wondering about what, where and when has all come down to the editing room. I am alive in the editing room. During the completion of this gift of love, I have cried, laughed, walked the studio floor, hugged everyone and most of all kept a heart full of prayer. The letters, the music, the sequence, the font, the direction and purpose all come from me. So far, we have laid the sound track, put in extra copy, built the necessary bridges and sequences of interviews. Mark and I are giving hundreds of hours and dedicating ourselves to a video we will both be proud of.

Without a net, I step out to do the true work I was called to do, and I am elated. As AIDS approaches, my pain is eased because of the work I've done to educate society. I see how many lives this video has already touched. All things are possible with God.

Telling people of my own and others' experience of learning about the virus, and the effects on women and families, has already proved to be a special gift for me. I will hold my head up. The issues of discrimination, rejection, isolation and harassment that my loving children could face are of great concern.

Disclosure is at hand.

Since HIV entered my life so rudely, my struggles have indeed been many. It has been a struggle to remain a mother, the central person in my children's lives, a struggle to hold on to a marriage plagued with alcohol and mistrust, a struggle to keep my health care status from company employees, a struggle to live with HIV and myelopathy, a struggle to contemplate the advance of AIDS in my once perfectly planned future.

January 27, 1996   This has been a week of one HIV/AIDS community meeting after another — the Tennessee AIDS Council, State Planning Group subcommittee meetings, Community Advisory Board meetings. All day, every day, someone talks about what to do. How help can best be given to rural/outer-city residents and metro/inner-city residents. How rural outlying communities suffer from a lack of acceptance, underfunded programs, and the constant fight to win monies from bigger communities. Populations in rural America have become infected in astronomical proportions.

People who live in the Bible Belt on farms or in small communities and who know everyone living within 300 miles don't think that HIV/AIDS could be a problem for them. The same small communities where ten-year-old girls get pregnant do not think that AIDS is their problem. The same small communities where STDs are seen throughout the school systems still think that HIV/AIDS is not their problem. The same small communities where, when asked, young teenagers say, "Yes, we are having unprotected sex." The numbers and facts are very clear; there is a problem.

How the ministers of these communities stand before their congregations with closed eyes, closed mouths and closed minds regarding the effects that HIV/AIDS is having on their congregations remains a mystery. Ministers, principals, teachers and leaders of these communities see the evidence. They have the disheartening figures staring them in the face. When outreach supporters ask that education be brought into their churches, country ministers have been known to say, "That sort of thing happens in big cities. It's not a problem out here in this small community."

Small-town America is not alone in this way of thinking. Big-city, metro-America seems to agree. The AIDS virus does not live among them; therefore it does not affect their lives. Where does HIV/AIDS live, if it does not live in small towns or big cities? The fact that so much denial exists in small communities, large communities, minority communities, women's communities, corporate communities and throughout the entire country is the exact reason for the increase in people acquiring HIV/AIDS. The country still sleeps. We are well into the second decade of HIV/AIDS, and America still sleeps. I feel so hopeless in the fight to try to get people to listen, to try to open minds and hearts to the reality of HIV. So many people whose lives have been touched in the most horrible way have tried for so many years, unsuccessfully, to reach out and deliver words of warning. The number of infections continues to escalate among humankind. How will I make a difference? Who is listening? HIV/AIDS is a world issue!

February 1, 1996 / Vaccine   Dr. William L. Moore Jr. is head of Communicable and Environmental Disease Control Services for the state of Tennessee. Dr. Moore told the Tennessee AIDS Council (I was present), "If a vaccine were found today, it would take two generations before an end point would be reached." He went on to say that he was being generous by saying two generations.

I found this news horrible. To me, that translates to my children and their children continuing to contract, live with and die from HIV/AIDS. It also tells me that two more generations will suffer discrimination, denial, disease and death caused by HIV/AIDS. Two more generations of mothers will worry for their children. At least two more generations will surrender to AIDS.

To further his statement, Dr. Moore said, "This is just the end point. It does not mean after two generations we're depleted, that the virus would not still be at epidemic levels." I sat in the room feeling disheartened, knowing that Dr. Moore had said "*if* a vaccine were found." Whether we agree or disagree with this statement, it can't help but make us think. The statement, right or wrong, definitely weighs heavy on me. Since my involvement in committees on the local, state, and federal levels, several things ring clear:

- One, HIV/AIDS numbers are increasing in every sector of society.
- Two, women and children don't stand a chance of reducing HIV infection until a loud and understandable message is heard in every ethnic culture of female society.
- Three, future generations will live with and die of HIV/AIDS.
- Four, bureaucracy begets bureaucracy.
- Five, money will always be at the root and will remain a strong factor in every facet of HIV/AIDS.

I see now why this epidemic is referred to as a "fight."

Vaccine research historically has received less funding than other areas of HIV/AIDS research. Although it may have been justified in the past, because little attention was paid to the "old ways of thinking," the spread of HIV and the growing number of infected persons trying different approaches to health care dictate a reassessment of priorities.

In poorer or underdeveloped countries, vaccines might be one of the only ways to prevent transmission and control the pathological consequences of infection. Poorer countries are also working hard to obtain treatments that restrict the spread of HIV/AIDS among their citizens. The world must organize a leadership structure directed at comprehensive vaccines. The United States has the tools necessary to accomplish this end. It would take some doing, but it could and should be done for all the world.

February 3, 1996 / Alcohol and Disappointment   My heart breaks as I watch the monster of alcohol give my babies such sorrow. My heart breaks as I see the decision I made a long time ago fade into divorce. Marrying Tim was supposed to be wonderful. It seemed the right thing to do because I loved him so deeply. I was truly happy, but it soon became short-lived happiness. Alcohol was showing up a lot, and I had no idea what the deal was.

I am alone in my home. The walls of protection surround me, only loosening to pick up one or all of my children and protect them from the evils of alcohol, from the hurt they must feel, from the hurt I feel. I have loved my husband as best I could. I have given until there is nothing left to give. I am alone in my home.

Years of trying to love it away and make excuses, accept excuses, have finally taken their toll. Disappointment is not good, yelling is not good, walking out is not good, belittling is not good.

Brandon and Jalyon sat around the house waiting for their father to take them sledding, but when he finally came home an hour and a half late, he told them, "No, I changed my mind." Aaron spent the night at Daniel's house. He told me, "Ma, I would rather stay at Daniel's house than wait on Daddy to disappoint me again."

February 10, 1996   Divorce seems my only choice.

February 17, 1996 / Obtaining HIV-Positive Results   Upon diagnosis, a person should get a skin test for tuberculosis (TB). TB is a bacterial infection that is caused by *Mycobacterium*. It is spread by airborne droplets inhaled through the nose or mouth and into the lungs. Healthy individuals usually have strong enough immune defenses to avoid getting TB. Vaccination with BCG (an attenuated strain of *M. tuberculosis*), still useful in certain parts of the world and in certain groups in which the prevalence of TB is high, is now rarely used in the United States.

This infection, when occurring in a person with immune suppression, must be watched by doctors and monitored with a simple skin test. A chest x-ray helps with diagnosis. It is very important to be tested for TB when diagnosed with HIV.

A test for syphilis, usually sexually transmitted, is also a wise decision. If a person has had unprotected sex, all STDs must be ruled out. Syphilis results from infection with the spirochete *Treponema pallidum*.

Testing for hepatitis B is also in order. Hepatitis is an inflammatory process in the liver. It can be caused by other viruses and by such things as alcohol abuse and certain drugs, legal or illegal, taken over several years. Today there are four major types of hepatitis: A, B, C and D. Each strain of hepatitis must be treated carefully with the right medications. Each hepatitis simplex virus must be monitored in HIV/AIDS patients, because hepatitis can lead to serious problems if not diagnosed and treated.

HIV/AIDS-positive women should have Pap smears every six months. Cervical cancers are on the rise for women who have tested positive. In the past, many women fell through the medical cracks and died of cervical cancer, but now we know that it is very important for women to get Pap smears and breast exams every six months, including women who have had hysterectomies. Unfortunately, most people have been conditioned to think of HIV/AIDS as affecting only certain groups. In the minds of those who are uninformed, women are one of the groups least likely to be affected. In fact, the way I was diagnosed shows how doctors can overlook and discount the possibility of women having HIV/AIDS. A large number of infected women are married or have been in significant relationships for years. Many of them have children and are in their childbearing years. Many are monogamous. Married women are mistakenly thought to be at very low risk of contracting HIV/AIDS. Again, it is thought that a married woman with no history of drug abuse, prostitution, or high-risk behavior stands a very small chance of becoming infected. But married women have no idea what their partners are doing when they are not around. At best, we can only hope that our partners are sincerely in love and faithful.

A big distinction between HIV-positive women and men is viral mutation in the genital tract. HIV-positive women have certain gynecological or genital tract conditions not found in men. These conditions may be harder to treat or may have a more accelerated course in HIV-positive women. An example is human papillomavirus (HPV). A woman who has HIV and HPV is more likely to have an inflamed cervix. This information strongly supports the need for Pap exams at the time of HIV diagnosis. Women suffer from this illness differently from men.

Many of us let our health care fall second, third or fourth behind whatever else is taking place in our lives. I am guilty of doing that very thing. Often other things take first place in my life, and I don't take certain medications prescribed by my doctors so that I can deal with family issues.

Dental care is another factor for HIV-positive people to look at. Cleaning and checkups are advised, because the mouth is an open invitation to all kinds of bacteria.

Counseling helped me tremendously when I was diagnosed. I recommend counseling and a good support group to anyone who gets a positive diagnosis. Having someone to trust and talk to helped give me mental stability in a time of emotional nightmares. It is believed by many in the HIV community that emotional-mental issues are as important as physical issues, and a well-rounded, coping HIV-positive person will have many mental issues to deal with throughout the rest of his or her life. I strongly recommend counseling for anyone diagnosed with HIV.

Doctors will take a complete medical history. At such time, they will ask questions about smoking, drinking, drugs and whatever habits one may have. Trying to change old behaviors and clean up one's act proves difficult at best, but considering small changes or one change at a time is better than changing one's life all at once. Breaking habits that have existed for years takes time and the desire to change. Change is difficult. Being diagnosed with HIV will bring about change. One way or another, HIV changes people. At best, it brings about good changes such as getting exercise, adopting better eating habits, including nutritional supplements, and taking care of oneself. I have learned that in order for me to take care of my wonderful, energetic children, I must take the time to nurture myself.

Upon diagnosis, we must begin, if we are not already doing so, to take care of ourselves and see to any unfinished business. Getting your house in order is what it is referred to.

February 18, 1996 / Women in Prison   Another aspect of HIV/AIDS that has received limited attention is treatment inside prison. Women in prison are not receiving proper medical treatment and are being released without the education necessary to take care of themselves. Many of those with life sentences are getting limited or no treatment.

This became clear to me while trying to find people to be interviewed for the video. Tennessee Prison for Women finally agreed, after repeated contact, to allow women inmates to write me letters.

We were not allowed access to do one-on-one interviews. I wanted to interview women in the system to get their reactions about the type of medical advice they were getting. The warden agreed to post a flyer I had written stating my reasons for wanting to receive letters.

In November 1995, I received a letter from a twenty-four-year-old mother of three who was doing time for child neglect. She wrote, "Shortly after having my third child, I became sexually involved with a female. After we were together two and a half years we found out that she was infected with the AIDS virus. It really scared me at first but I had no fear in dying. I felt like if it was meant for me to catch the virus, then I would. I am not scared of people who are infected because they are still human and all people should be treated equally." She went on to say, "There are a lot of people in your condition whose families turn against them, especially when they are in a place like this. I know about this firsthand because my girlfriend's family turned on her when she told them. Family members are slow to come here anyway, and show little support to a lot of us in here." Her letter went on to say how grateful she was to know that someone on the outside wanted to hear from inmates who were HIV-positive. She wrote "Don't be fooled. Sex is an every-day occurrence in here. Women are having multi-sex encounters with each other and with corrections officers all the time."

At the time I received her letter, this woman did not know if she was infected, because she had not been tested while incarcerated. She was afraid of the treatment she had seen other HIV-positive inmates receive — treatment she described as inhuman — from both corrections officers and fellow inmates. Stigma and discrimination in the system itself make it difficult for change to occur.

Another letter I received in January 1996 said, "I'm a mother of two little girls and have been in here for over two years. I hope to get out soon. I found out I was infected in here. My T-cell count is 293 and they want me to take something called AZT. I don't know what that stuff is, but the doctor told me I would be taking it. I don't know much about AZT, HIV or AIDS, and the infor-mation I have now does not help. I don't dare tell anyone in here except those in the medical department and the warden because I would be treated as an outcast. This is already a horrible place to be but could be a whole lot worse if others learned of my infection. I was glad to see your flyer posted, maybe you can send me some information. Believe me, whatever you send will be more than I have now." I sent her a large envelope full of information that I hoped would be helpful.

February 27, 1996 / "Reasons to Live: Women, Their Families and HIV"   It's taken a year of my life to put this labor of love together. There are some things I would have done better, but a year has gone into this work, and a feeling of blessedness overwhelms me.

HIV has taken its toll on many of those appearing in "Reasons to Live." Roxanne is sicker. Deidre is retiring from Nashville Cares at the ripe old age of twenty-six. She can no longer do all the traveling it takes to speak to the many, many church groups, community groups, rallies and fund-raisers she has attended over the past two years. Her T-cell count is in the single digits. She's lost so much weight. Every effort is being made for her to gain weight, but she continues to lose it. We both know it's the wasting syndrome, and we cried together on the phone as we discussed her symptoms. We talked about Elsa.

Wasting syndrome is the involuntary loss of 10 percent or more of baseline body weight, complicated by bouts of diarrhea and weakness.

Deidre was the first black woman I met with AIDS. She, along with Lisa, held me together when I was diagnosed. Back then, she possessed a spunky, confident personality. Today she's still confident, still matter-of-fact. I love Deidre spiritually.

For me, HIV still keeps lymph nodes swollen throughout my body. I had another major seizure recently. Southern Hills Hospital sent me home when I told them that I was HIV-positive, doing little to treat me. Myelopathy symptoms continue, and my stamina dwindles. Numbness from the surgery still exists, but I can stand upright.

Tim's refusal to deal with how HIV was introduced into our marriage, his years of alcohol abuse, and his unwillingness to respect my opinion have given me reasons to dissolve what was once my marriage. *Recovery through compassion.*

Our marriage, in the beginning, consisted of shared values and shared ideas and goals. Things changed throughout the years as alcohol changed his way of thinking. At first I thought that I could love away alcohol. I just knew that if I kept loving and giving in to his way of dealing with things, he would change. Not.

Since his diagnosis, Tim's alcoholism and the behaviors that accompany it have progressed. He drinks more and more. Happiness means a drink, sadness means a drink and everything becomes a drink or a reason to drink. It is not easy to give up your soul mate because of alcoholism and HIV. Hiding his drinking from me was always something he tried to do but was never successful at. Soon he could not hide it from the children either.

I look forward to the peace of mind and the healing my children and I will find.

February 28, 1996   The situation with the company intensifies, and my concerns grow. Seems to me that management has really done a poor job keeping in line with the Americans with Disabilities Act.

March 2, 1996 / Disclosure in the Family   I decided that it is time for other family members to know about the guarded secret. I can no longer keep the facts of HIV from my family in Michigan. The reason for keeping it so hush-hush had to do with protecting my mother from family gossip. It was important to my mother that no one in the family be informed. She has no idea that I told Lee Lee over a year ago, but she will find out soon. Lee Lee and I decided that her parents should be told. As Lee and I discussed their reaction to the news, I asked how she would tell them. She said that her mother and father were up visiting her for the weekend, and this would be a good time to inform them. I told her to go for it. Family support is what Lee has given me in the changing uncertainties of HIV. She said that the video would be a good tool to use, along with all the newspaper articles, advertisements and letters I've sent her over the past year.

We weighed the consequences of telling her parents. How will they react? Will they respond like my mother always said they would? Who else in the family will they tell? Should they be asked not to say anything to my mother? All the questions seemed irrelevant until that one came out. I can't live with the secret anymore.

I can't continue to do the work I do and live with the family secret. I can't continue to do the work I do within the HIV/AIDS community and betray my own beliefs. It is a tremendous relief now that the guarded family secret is no longer kept under wraps. Protecting my mother from family shame, as I see it, is no longer an option, because I've got tough decisions to make, and I can't change my mother. I am a single mother with three underaged children. A question I now consider is who will care for them when I am too sick. Who will take on the responsibilities of parenting my children when I can no longer care for them? My wonderful friends will do what they can, I know, but I must look at the long-term situation. Single parenting finds me having to deal with issues that I didn't anticipate as a married woman. Tim and I had talked about what we would do when one of us got sick. As always, the other would step in and take the lead while keeping things going. Getting sick at the same time was pretty much unacceptable behavior. Now I must regroup. I find it easier to eliminate people rather than wondering who I can count on in the long term. I can't help but think that other people with terminal illnesses who are alone have given great thought to some of these same issues. These decisions will have to be made soon, because HIV, myelopathy and seizures have become a constant reminder that HIV continues to thrive within me, and decisions for the children's care must be made.

I haven't written about myelopathy. I put it in my God box.

March 16, 1996
My Children,

It seems as though we advocates and activists are failing in attempts to educate. Today my mind is filled with thoughts about losses. As little Deondra lies sick in the Vanderbilt Children's Hospital AIDS ward, I think about how we are losing our young to AIDS. How we are losing our major workforce to AIDS. How we are losing the fight with government and AIDS in the military. How we are losing our fight with insurance companies that think it's right to take people's insurance away at a time when it is needed the most. How we are losing the HIV/AIDS fight to money. It seems more important to have money and power. HIV/AIDS is not

Tell the children
Tell them that HIV is real
Tell them that AIDS is real
We are losing too many children
Show them how to protect themselves
Use words like condoms, abstinence, risk behaviors.
Show them that it does not have to happen
Save one, save many.
Call out to the young of the world, we are all affected
Mothers, fathers, brothers, sisters tell the young ones,
    we are all touched.
Educate minds with knowledge that empowers.
Use tools of compassion, concern, promise for strong
    intelligence which grows in the hearts of children.
You must tell the children of the consequences of
    HIV/AIDS.

going away, and until it comes home to the White House, Congress and Senate, we continue to fight, sometimes seemingly in vain.

I wish for this virus never to touch another human. I wish for this virus to be wiped from the face of this earth. I wish people would listen and learn from those of us trying to deliver a message of such great importance.

Only the creative mind of God knows the future.

March 26, 1996 I just returned from four days in Rockville, Maryland, attending another CCG committee meeting. I've learned a lot about political policies, pharmaceutical companies, HIV and the military, which AIDS organizations will be funded and which ones won't. I learned about my fellow committee members and their commitment to the CCG. Sadly, bureaucracy is everywhere; unfortunately, though understandably, it's even in the CCG. It's termed "playing the game, getting with the program." Playing the bureaucracy game sucks. People with AIDS are dying. That's all I want to keep shouting to everyone. The CCG members I serve with are all infected or affected. Men and women, black and white, straight and gay, married and single, serve together for the common good. One person has a son with HIV, and he himself is also positive. His wife has already died of an AIDS-related illness. Another person has adopted two children, one white and one black, who are infected. Another's husband is infected, and so is she. Some work full time in hospitals around the country, and others operate organizations that work with HIV/AIDS adults and/or children. A young woman travels from New York but must return before the conference is over because she starts a new clinical trial. One man lives in Hawaii and was so moved by the video that he cried when he saw it. Yes, it was shown at the joint CCG-Patient Care meeting.

While learning about all that is wrong with HIV/AIDS and the government, I have also given thought to where in this catastrophic pandemic black women are. Black women in America make up the largest population of new infections. As I see it, we, myself included, must continue to be strong to endure all that is life's pain. The black women I know are strong, independent, self-knowing sisters — sisters who stand, sisters who take a stand, sisters who are sisters to the end. They open their minds and let fresh air fill their hearts, allowing a free soul to take flight, working to improve people through educating children and others. Together we feel the devastation of our future generations becoming infected with HIV/AIDS. We see firsthand the children, young lives succumbing to AIDS. We see women, black women, doing nothing to protect themselves from HIV.

Changing the behavior of women has proved difficult due to cultural norms, addictions, abuse, homelessness, coping mechanisms, lack of self-esteem, sexual addictions, maintaining family unity, partners' unwillingness to use protection during sex, wanting babies, financial security, emotional attachment to partners, same-sex relationships, delay between behaviors and consequences, not considering contraceptive use after giving birth, few alcohol and drug centers available, early sexual experiences, loneliness in old age, escape through sex, sexual spontaneity, ignorance of partners' risk, unclean needles, partners using drugs, ignoring symptoms, feeling unlovable, belief that anal sex requires no protection, willingness to perform oral sex without protection, sex for money, mimicking parents' behaviors, belief that AIDS is a gay male disease, severe and persistent mental illness, and basic denial of infection. Most of these issues are untouched by a lot of us, but we women see others live with unbelievable issues. However, building positive relationships with as many women as possible has shown significant results. If you spend some time helping others, it helps you in the long run.

While I've seen and heard a lot, I think of my mother. How she gives little support to me. How I still wish I had my mother's support. How I wish she had educated herself and learned about the illness that lives in her daughter. I tell her nothing about seizures, biopsies or the ills of HIV. Having my mother's support while divorcing Tim would have been nice and less lonely. She's still unaware that I told Lee Lee about HIV. I am glad that someone else in the family knows besides my mother and my brother. I am glad that I can share HIV with a member of my family, grateful to have Lee Lee, though she doesn't replace my mother, but I am grateful. I must work on my relationship with my mother. Though it is hard for us to communicate, I know that she is still there for the kids. She continues to call, send gifts and visit. She loves the children to pieces.

March 30, 1996   So many changes have occurred over the short time since I filed for divorce. I am learning how to think like a single mother. I am working on healing inner values and regaining my self-respect. WORTH.

The process of mourning different stages of loss, welcomed or unwelcomed, is indeed a process. It moves slowly, depending on the person, or fast, depending on the depth of loss. While reflecting, my life is moving ever so quickly. Two different lifestyles later, my life has changed; my faith has changed; I have changed, and those closest to me have begun to notice. I am more fulfilled in my work, more fulfilled in my relationships with my children. Now I can smile. Now I can see that I have changed my destiny.

Faith fills my heart. Love fills the spaces between pain and my future, although I am well aware of the effects HIV still has on me. The myelopathy affects even more parts of my body, and fatigue still has me unable to get out of bed at times.

While we are left to rebuild our lives, my mind keeps coming back to the biopsy I am scheduled for next week. Two years have done little to heal one area of my stomach, so Dr. Richard has scheduled a removal of skin to be tested. I actually thought that my plate was full, but it seems I must somehow set aside room for the possibilities of the results of these tests.

It hurts me again that the kids must worry about me. Aaron's calling every day from school since I told him; Brandon's hanging out around me; Jalyon's under foot. The divorce isn't easy for them, either.

April 6, 1996   Easter is tomorrow. I am remembering Easter two years ago, when Tim took me to the hospital, which was the beginning of change for each member of this house.

April 11, 1996   Tomorrow is the two-year anniversary of HIV's entrance into my life. This year seems to be worse than the first. I think it may have to do with not being with Tim. I believe that HIV/AIDS is no blessing. I believe that blessings come from good, not bad. I believe that evil caused HIV/AIDS and that all blessings are good, and nothing is good about HIV/AIDS. Blessings that have occurred in my life since diagnosis have come from good and the growth I have accomplished over the past two years. Growth most often is painful, but HIV changes one's perspective. Somehow it becomes time to prioritize and settle unfinished business, work on quality-of-life issues and ditch the garbage.

April 21, 1996 / Sarratt Cinema Susan Ford Wiltshire had arranged for beautiful flowers to be placed at the podium where I was to speak. The theater was abuzz with college students, young laughter and conversation. As the hour grew near, the seats began to fill. The audience was a mixture of college students, professors, doctors, business administrators, nursing staff and students, young and the young at heart, white, black, Hispanic, Latin, poor and the very affluent — all were present. My children were seated in the audience as well.

I sat overcome with tears as audience members' eyes were glued to the screen. "Reasons to Live: Women, Their Families and HIV" was received better than I had hoped. Tennessee Congressmen Fred Thompson and Bob Clement had been sent invitations, as well as Nashville's Mayor Phil Bredesen. The only one to respond favorably to his invitation was Senator Bill Frisk. He sent a kind letter saying that he would be out of town and would be unable to attend personally, but a staff member would attend. State director Emily J. Reynolds came up to me after the half-hour question-and-answer portion to inform me that Senator Frisk sent his deepest regrets and that his office was more than willing to help combat HIV/AIDS in Tennessee. Ms. Reynolds suggested that I contact her directly for any assistance.

The most important part of the evening for me, personally, was when Aaron raised his hand and thanked me for educating him, his sister and brother. I began to cry on stage in front of everyone. I am honored to know that my children are proud of me, and being thanked publicly for educating through speeches, letters and the video touched me deeply. I've agonized over allowing my children to attend public appearances. As their mother, my concern for how they will be treated will remain, but I see that it is indeed time for my children to rise to their own challenges of having a mother with HIV who speaks publicly.

So much of my time is spent with education, meetings, planning, conference calls, producing yet another video and organizing WOMEN (see below) that I had begun to feel that my children were being neglected, but no words were more meaningful to me that night than the words from my son.

April 22, 1996 / Founder and Executive Director of an AIDS Organization   Two years later, I find myself the founder of WOMEN, Women on Maintaining Education and Nutrition. Life has sure changed, hasn't it? Together, Bobbi Lee, Deidre and I got WOMEN afloat. Deidre has many wonderful ideas about using resources we already have in the state. Bobbi Lee has many ideas about ways to work WOMEN. The three of us will make a difference in women's lives because we care, because we are HIV-positive and well aware of the needs of women.

WOMEN is a grassroots organization whose mission is to target women and their families who are both infected and affected by HIV/AIDS. WOMEN's purpose is to provide appropriate education, both culturally and gender specifically.

Growth is at hand.

"Reasons to Live: Women, Their Families and HIV" will be shown at a convention in Guyana and will also be seen in Switzerland in July. The video's gone global.

While remaining on sick leave because HIV changed my life's work, my salary has decreased tremendously, but I am happier. The company's stated philosophy contains many truths, such as that all employees want to be involved in decisions that affect them, care about their jobs, take pride in themselves and in their contributions and want to share in the success of their efforts. It talks about creating an atmosphere of mutual trust and respect, the recognition and utilization of individual expertise in innovative ways, providing the technologies and education for each individual. In this way, the company hopes to enjoy successful relationships with employees and develop a sense of belonging to an integrated business system capable of achieving common goals that ensure security for employees and success for the business and local communities.

When I come to the end of light and
I step out into the nothingness of darkness
I will step into faith.
Faith is knowing either there is something solid
   in the darkness
or I will learn how to fly.
Catch me.

The company also proclaims that its mission is to market products developed and manufactured in the United States that are world leaders in quality, cost and customer enthusiasm through the integration of people, technology and business systems.

These words are found in company documents given to each "team member" upon hiring. But it seems to me that the implementation of the mission statement falls short in its integration of people, technology, and business systems departments. Instead, employees and their families must harbor silence and suffer loss at the workplace as well. Workplaces and churches are a large part of life. Earning a living for one's family is what we all want, including those of us living with a catastrophic, life-threatening illness.

7:30 P.M.   Deidre's health is of concern to us all. She is now taking Crixivan, a new medication. She called me recently and said that she was experiencing dizziness, confusion, loss of hearing in one ear, no number recall and an unexplained euphoric high.

Crixivan, or indinavir sulfate, is a new type of anti-HIV drug known as an HIV protease inhibitor. Crixivan fights HIV by blocking the virus from producing new viruses that get released in the body. Taking Crixivan with other anti-HIV drugs or by itself can also help lower the amount of HIV circulating in the bloodstream (viral load). Crixivan has shown evidence of increasing the number of CD4 cells, or raising T-cell counts. However, it is critical to take Crixivan exactly as prescribed. Taking less Crixivan than prescribed or skipping doses can make it less effective and may eventually lead to drug-resistant forms of HIV emerging in the body. Crixivan is not a cure for AIDS. People taking this drug may continue to develop opportunistic infections and other complications associated with HIV. Crixivan has not been shown to reduce the incidence or frequency of such illnesses. Long-term effects of Crixivan are unknown, and therein lies my personal concern. It has not been proved to reduce the risk of transmission of HIV to others through sexual contact or blood contamination.

The side effects of Crixivan include nephrolithiasis, flank pain, blood in the urine, kidney stones, nausea, abdominal pain, headache, diarrhea, vomiting, weakness or fatigue, insomnia, taste changes, acid regurgitation and back pain.

Deidre and her doctor think that drinking coffee was a contributing factor to her symptoms. Supposedly, Crixivan can be taken with many of the approved drugs used to treat people with HIV. However, taking terfenadine, astemizole, cisapride, triazolam or midazolam with Crixivan is not recommended by its manufacturer.

Looking over reports, I find myself concerned about the fact that Crixivan has not been sufficiently studied in women due to constraints on availability. Cervical dysplasia studies have not been sufficiently done; therefore, what this drug does to women's reproductive organs is basically unknown. Again, women's bodies become a big issue. Clinical trials, for the most part, involve women these days, but women have historically been dismissed from trials if they become pregnant or are in their childbearing years. Many women do not want to enter clinical trials because of the past history of such trials. And studies are unclear on the effects on women.

Deidre was so happy to receive her UPS shipment of Crixivan, because she now has only two T-cells and was not taking any medications. She is very frail and has lost well over 20 percent of her body weight. Her spunk is still intact, and she gets around town in her bright red sports car as often as she can. She's not down yet. Bobbi Lee and I are very grateful for her contributions to WOMEN.

April 24, 1996   The Ebola virus was reported to have come ashore in the United States. Two monkeys have died from Ebola, and others were said to be in quarantine. The media report no cause for alarm, but remember this day. In my opinion, we will hear more about Ebola in the United States. How this country thinks that it is an exception to universal law escapes me. That, in part, is why HIV/AIDS was allowed to spread so quietly. The United States is not exempt from anything. We in this great country are no better than any other people. Ebola and other plagues can occur here, just as they occur in other countries.

April 25, 1996   I am not well today. Utter fatigue has hit me, and movement is difficult. I am having some lung congestion, headache, and much myelopathy pain. A rash has developed along the side of my neck and face. I will spend today in bed, unable to interact with the kids, other than their coming to my room to spend time with me. It seems it's time to contact the doctor's office for an appointment. I guess it's time for me to know what my T-cell count is and where I am exactly in this virus.

April 26, 1996 / Ultimately Alone   She was a middle-aged woman around forty-three, well educated and knowledgeable of her surroundings. Victoria had many friends who died of AIDS, and she nursed several of them. Death was no stranger to her, as she served her community as a volunteer. Victoria was a chef by profession. Preparing meals in elegant fashion, she often gave her talent to HIV/AIDS patients. Victoria had AIDS, but no one knew. Because she worked endlessly helping others, Victoria learned how to cover up lesions that appeared on her face and body, how to cover those unsightly herpes outbreaks. Because she saw how those she helped were treated, Victoria was determined not to let rejection happen to her. She quickly taught herself how to apply makeup to unsightly lesions, how to excuse herself when she knew she was about hurl food prepared by friends and loving family members. Though she was a chef, she rarely ate. Never did anyone see the medications she hid. When she was too sick to get out of bed, Victoria would simply not answer the telephone, and the answering machine would say, "Sorry, I'm busy helping others at the moment, please leave a message and I will be happy to help you too."

For years, Victoria hid behind her work. She gave herself to service work seven days a week. Tirelessly, she buried friends, feeling each loss with deep emotion, choosing not to share her own HIV status with anyone. She appeared strong, healthy and knowledgeable about social and political issues. Her advice was sought by leaders of her community.

When I met Victoria near the end of her life, she told me about the sorrow she felt for those family members and friends who would reject her. "I felt the only way I could remain loved was not to tell anyone. Everyone knew I worked and cared for AIDS patients, but in that work, I learned that rejection from those you love the most is very real. I saw families torn apart with news of HIV/AIDS."

"Vicky, I am so sorry you have felt you must carry your burden alone," I told her. "Why me, Vic, why tell me what has happened to you all these years?"

"Because the time has come for disclosure. Because I know my time has come to die."

Victoria heard me on the Fisk radio interview I gave last year and contacted me through Nashville Cares' Heartline. After listening to me share my story, she told me, "There was something you said that impressed me. Your words of discrimination, disclosure and family rejection stayed with me. I heard you say you have three children, and I realized your courageousness for talking publicly about your life with HIV."

During that conversation, Victoria told me about the Saturday afternoon she had sat alone in her apartment making decisions about her personal possessions — who she wanted to have her favorite dress, who was to have the antique dresser, the china she had brought back from Europe, and the most prized possession she owned, her cat. How she wanted her funeral to be and who was to give her eulogy. Written instructions for every detail were safely tucked away in her Bible. She told her closest friend, Candice, that if anything happened to her, remember the Bible. She attended the premiere of "Reasons to Live: Women, Their Families and HIV" that was held at Vanderbilt's Sarratt Cinema and greeted me with encouraging wisdom. She said that she admired all that I've accomplished with "Reasons." Victoria died alone that Friday night of AIDS-related cervical cancer. She chose to serve her community for as long as she could. She chose not to tell her mother, because she had heard her mother say, "None of my children better not ever tell me they got AIDS, cause I'll disown 'em."

Vic and I shared life stories of defending our sexuality to others. We spoke of job discrimination, workplace policy for infected employees, and helping humanity understand life with HIV/AIDS. Many conversations later, Victoria found a renewed spiritual level she felt comfortable with.

We shared how religious beliefs had changed for us both. How spirituality was something we had had to confront, and where exactly we stood in the larger picture of life.

She's gone ahead of me to start the work her higher power has for her. I know that she will stay busy, because that is what makes her happiest. Since Victoria's death, my heart has another small piece missing. I feel her presence and know that she does not suffer. Her warm, loving voice awaits me. As I go about my life, doing the work Vic and I were called to do, I know that I have indeed touched one earthly life with that work.

April 27, 1996 I've taken the path of knowledge instead of the path of denial — choosing to empower self through positive motion but knowing the ever-presence of HIV. The end is uncomfortably closer because of HIV/AIDS, but I don't see an end to the work I do. When I leave, I am now confident that my children will carry on with my work, that their hearts and spirit will lead them in their own personal mission toward inner growth and spiritual wealth.

Sex education Although sex education programs in schools have been around for many years, most programs have not been nearly effective enough. Schools should take a rigorous look at their programs and begin implementing innovative programs that have been proved effective. Parents, educators and policy makers must work together to avoid misconceptions about sex education to reduce the rates of unwanted pregnancies and STDs, which are on the rise among American youth. Young people, parents, teachers and schools must be integral partners in developing and delivering HIV prevention programs for adolescents. We can no longer ignore the need for education both on how to postpone sexual involvement and how to protect oneself when sexually active. Comprehensive risk-prevention programs using multiple elements are needed to protect as many of those at risk for pregnancy and STD/HIV infection as possible. Based on current information provided by the CDC, an average of two young people are infected with HIV every hour of every day. The rate of HIV infection becomes apparent from the number of young adults diagnosed with AIDS. Unfortunately, our children are a generation at risk.

It is unlikely that we will be with our children when they face the decision whether or not to have sex. The idea of their children even thinking about such things causes some parents to get upset. However, our children do think about sex and drugs. If we talk openly at home about making wise decisions, we can help them resist peer pressure and make informed choices that will help protect their health now and for the rest of their lives. It does indeed take a village.

Knowledge is not enough to change behaviors. Programs that focus on helping teenagers change their behaviors by using role playing, skits, games and creative exercises that strengthen social skills have shown signs of success. Often, health education pertaining to sexuality begins in high school, but by then, many students have already begun experimenting sexually. Giving teenagers the tools they need in life requires HIV education.

May 25, 1996   During the time since my last entry, I have continued counseling with Joan, helped Bobbi Lee move, filled many videotape requests, had our family portrait taken (which was a big job), attended Ryan White focus groups, done another television interview, replaced items Tim took when he moved out, prepared for the children's summer, completed plans for "Reasons" to appear on a community-access network locally and wrote the agenda for the first scheduled WOMEN's board meeting, after being successful at recruiting a strong group of individuals to be board members. I had lunch with Jalyon at school and tried to keep my financial head above water.

Personal care   I've been learning about holistic treatments while continuing my education on current protocols, and I'm comfortable with my nurtured health care regimen. The myelopathy pain still exists, but I am trying a new medication, so we'll see. I have a massage twice a month, check in with my mental health specialist, write, do several speaking engagements per week, fully represent WOMEN as its executive director, do outreach in the community, spend quality time with the children, plan the second video, stay close to friends, close doors on relationships that cause T-cell loss and stay current with my medical journal, which I have given to a close friend.

May 26, 1996 / My Children's Reaction to HIV
Brandon   "It doesn't feel any different having an HIV-positive mother. She's still my mom and still runs my life. When I was

asked by other teenagers, my age, how it feels to have an HIV-positive mother, my answer was and is, I don't feel any difference. She's my mom. Yes, she's been sick plenty of times and I worry about that, but she gets better and continues to lay down the law, even from her hospital bed."

Aaron   "I feel blessed because I understand the ways to get HIV now. I understand ways not to get it too. I've learned that everyone can get HIV, that no one is immune. I used to feel it wasn't a part of my life, that it was always somebody else's life. But now I know you can't live and always think it's somebody else or that it won't happen in your home, to someone you love. It can. It happened in my home to my mom, a person I never thought could get HIV. I feel sad sometimes knowing she could die, but today my mom is healthy and today I have my mom."

Jalyon   "I feel better now because I have had time to become closer to my mother, we talk more about her feelings and mine. I travel with her when she speaks to groups. Sometimes they ask me questions about living with an HIV-positive mother. At first I didn't know what HIV was and I was scared when Mom told me, because I thought I would get HIV. I felt sad, scared and worried cause Mom told me she could die from it. Explaining really didn't ease my worry at the time, but I was comfortable in my mother's arms. My mom explained that I couldn't get HIV from her by drinking after her, hugging her, kissing her or touching her. Boy, that was a relief, 'cause she's my mom and I will always hug, kiss and touch her."

11:30 P.M.   Deidre's ill.

I've been so busy with change and caring for sick friends that there's been little time for anything else. I've spoken at several community centers in the area. Low-income housing areas are often left out of outreach efforts. Those that were present at yesterday's event were sparked to conversation and thought, which is what I am trying to get them to do. Thinking before acting can make a difference.

My heart is filled with concern for the children in those rooms — young hormones waiting to experience their first sexual encounter, making decisions about drug use and whether or not to have sex, feeling love from a boyfriend or girlfriend for the first time. These choices are critical for young people. They also can be hard decisions for mature adults who face the dating game. Adults who already use drugs and whose minds are clouded must find it difficult not to do drugs, but HIV/AIDS education must continue, encouraging help for addictions and finding strength within.

Paul, a friend of mine, was addicted to crack cocaine for over fifteen years. His life went from a wonderful home and family in the 'burbs to losing everything, including his family, and becoming infected with HIV. Sharing needles was a common occurrence for him and those he got high with. Time passed, and Paul cleaned up. He shares with young preteens and teens his story of active addiction, giving details of how life was and the endless cycle of addiction he finally broke. Paul seems content to tell youngsters about his past, comparing himself to where he is today. HIV-positive with three past opportunistic infections, Paul jumps on opportunities to tell children about life inside active addiction and HIV.

June 4, 1996   Today my marriage of ten years came to an end. I feel like hell. Now I have to face life as an HIV-positive mother alone with three children.

Divorce hearings were over in less time than it took to get there — ten years over in less than ten minutes. Tim was a no-show, as expected, and a hearing date for property settlement was scheduled.

June 6, 1996   Deidre, Bobbi Lee and I had a directors' meeting today. Deidre is very ill. She's still losing weight and very weak. She spent our meeting lying flat on her back on the floor.

June 12, 1996   The children and I are in the mountains today. The drive to east Tennessee was wonderful. The room overlooks the in-ground pool, a pond, a volleyball court and a vista of breathtaking mountains. I'm here for a State Planning Group retreat to discuss the upcoming 1997 budget for our state. I still find it difficult to plan money allocations for state programs based on CDC guidelines. Every agency, it is hoped, wants to do a good job and have money to accomplish goals. It saddens me to know that money is the starting and ending point for programs while HIV infections occur continuously throughout the state, throughout the country, throughout the world. However, I will enjoy these days in the mountains. I will take time to become one with them. The mountains bring me peace. The children will have a good time fishing, swimming and hanging out with the other children who have come.

June 20, 1996   Deidre and I finished an interview with a local cable network today.

June 22, 1996   "Reasons" makes it to television. I am filled with emotion as the children and I view it.

July 20, 1996   I haven't written in a while because I am computer bound, working on turning these words into a book for Kumarian Press. While constructing pieces of the past two years, I have had to relive my life, my family's life, inside HIV/AIDS.

Several women I know who are living with or have died from HIV/AIDS got their first OI during the second year of diagnosis. I take their advice in trying to take care of myself.

Node swelling continues, and some type of infection is happening. Pus runs from orifices of my body. Abdominal skin still has no feeling. Double vision and dizziness have been going on for the last two days.

July 22, 1996   I mailed the completed manuscript to Kumarian Press today, but I will keep writing.

July 23, 1996   Property settlement day. Again, Tim was a no-show.

July 31, 1996   Jalyon and I are leaving tomorrow for home after seven wonderful educational days in Washington, D.C. For Jalyon, it was a time of learning more about policies and AIDS. She met CCG members, who became surrogate moms and dads, friends who showed her unconditional acceptance, people she accepted without judgment, women and men who spent time taking her to the zoo, downtown D.C. on the Metro and an exciting rally on welfare reform. Jalyon saw thousands of people, heard the issues of welfare reform and met ACT-UP supporters. She even saw people get arrested. She learned that Americans are angry about basic needs being taken away.

At ten years old, I don't think she understands the reasoning behind the anger, but she does know that people are mad. Jalyon told me, "Momma, I just stood there saying I'm at the White House, I'm really here. Thanks, Mom, for bringing me." It gives me great pleasure to know that my daughter was able to experience so many historic sights as well as current events. My wonderful friends care about the community in which they live and care for the children of the community. They are community advocates who make a difference and care for America's future generations.

My time in Washington was spent in meetings learning more about protocol regulations, protocol structures, monotherapy versus combination therapy, new medications still in development. Physicians from across the country gave updates on trial results and patient care concerns. I learned how HIV has affected other CCG members' lives. A former IV drug user shared how important it is for the CCG to remain focused on not excluding those who use drugs. He went on to say, "Those that use have sex too." Most of his comments ended with, "We can't be exclusive to any class." We, the CCG, came to Washington from diverse backgrounds and represented a wide variety of the population we serve.

Faith is acting upon belief — not just believing, but truly acting upon one's belief in a positive way. Because HIV eyes see faith, I act upon my belief that *everyone* should be educated and that education should be as natural as nutrition is for the body. Faith is that which is unseen but is absolute.

Grief is a reaction frequently felt because of the great losses encountered by HIV-positive patients. Relationships with family members lost to HIV/AIDS give reason for deep feelings of grief. Close and even distant friends who have died of AIDS-related illness, rejection from family or rejection from a romantic, thought-to-be-lasting relationship, all these can cut you with feelings of grief and mourning.

Webster's dictionary says that grief is deep sorrow, a cause of sorrow or anxiety, a disaster. How often do we think that we have met with disaster? How many times must we feel sorrow? How often the heartbreak in the wake of HIV/AIDS!

August 1, 1996 / Conversation among HIV Friends "I'm twenty-six years old. AIDS made me grow up far faster than my peers and my ex-husband. My viral load is 80,000 since taking norvir. T cells are at three at last count. If they go up at next visit I'll schedule a T-cell party to celebrate."

Deidre told me about her second OI and her recent stay in Vanderbilt's hospital. Her last stay at Vanderbilt began June 30, 1996. At the time, she was diagnosed with brain encephalitis coupled with dementia. She was not herself. She wasn't self-destructive or violent, but her personality was deeply altered. She was behaving very insensitively toward others; she heard and saw things, taking them literally, unable to separate the real from the imagined. Things were cloudy, but others have since helped her recall and fill in some of the blank spots in her memory.

She recalls that the emergency room doctor was quick to medicate her. The emergency room caregivers knew nothing of her history. The physician had just arrived two days before and was still learning the policies and procedures of Vanderbilt's emergency room. "Luck would have it that way," she said. At the time this happened, none of Deidre's medical support was available to aid with history or diagnosis. Her doctor was out of town, as was the nurse-practitioner in charge of her case. It was late at night, and the HIV clinic was closed. The emergency room doctor immediately diagnosed her as psychotic without knowing anything about her or the medications she was on. She said, "They should have waited until the clinic opened the next morning before administering any meds. They should have tried to confirm the medications I was taking, but they didn't, Catherine, they didn't." Friends who accompanied her to the emergency room told the staff of her symptoms. Deidre rattled off her list of medications, but they seemed to fall on deaf ears. The doctor didn't know that antipsychotic medications should not be given with protease inhibitors without checking. It seems he didn't know enough about AIDS drugs. He didn't know enough about AIDS to wait. "It wasn't a life-threatening situation, I wasn't going to

Photo: Duane Brown

Deidre Williams.

kill myself or anybody else, none of my vital organs were hanging out, I wasn't bleeding. If they thought I was a danger to others, they could have put me in a padded room until they found out better.

"Catherine," she went on to say, "this is America, and if you have a problem, we have a pill to solve it." The health care team gave Deidre Haldol without Cogentin, which is administered with Haldol to offset its side effects. The Haldol was administered alone. "It locked me up. I couldn't move my mouth. My speech was very deliberate and slow. Catherine, that Monday night I think I died. I went to a place in my mind that I clearly remember having never been. If it wasn't death, it was closer than I've ever been. I lost control of my bowels, I urinated all over myself. I was in a room that was situated in front of the nurses' station. It was a dark, small, closet-like room with a mattress on the floor. There was no view of a clock, no window, nothing. I was placed on the mattress. I was hurting. Before I went into this room, they gave me a shot of Benadryl, then made me take my protease inhibitor." Norvir should not be taken with sleeping medication or antihistamines unless prescribed by an HIV/AIDS specialist.

"I recall the nurse coming in and saying, 'We have to clean her up.' I remember that statement clearly. They moved me from the mattress, cleaned it and returned me to the same mattress. I remember in my mind, I don't know what they were doing with my body, but I was going down a tunnel. At first I didn't see a light, then it started becoming brighter, then I started seeing people that I knew. I saw Frederick Douglass, Malcolm X and a cluster of people that were already dead. I saw David, a friend's husband who passed away two years ago from AIDS." As Deidre talked, I began to feel her reality. Days later, she had been able to sneak to a phone and call me. I remembered her voice trembling as she spoke softly to me. I remembered not wanting to get off the phone, but she had to hang up when a nurse was heard approaching.

Deidre said, "The second time I almost died and went into an altered state of consciousness, I saw the big light. There was a gate to the light, and people were sitting around waiting for their turn to enter into the light. It was very peaceful, and I knew it was good. I never got close enough to the gate to enter into the light, but the warmth of the light lifted me. Catherine," she said, "the second time I was not afraid."

Later — she couldn't recall when — she was moved to a room where the walls were gray, the floor was a bland color. The room had a window with a mesh covering but no view, no clock. She told time by the sun. Today she wakes by the sun.

Her parents came, and she begged them to get her out. Her parents were not allowed to take her. She told her mother that she wanted to be out by the Fourth of July. Her mother told her, "No, dear, it's July 6." At that point in our conversation, she broke down and began to cry. She did not know that so much time had passed.

Deidre told me, "Catherine, the support team you have mustn't leave you. It can be done in shifts or whatever, but it is very important that someone stay with you at all times. If they have to sleep in a chair, so be it. You should have support that supports and doesn't freak out. Save the drama for later. The support team has to remain calm and take control of your health care and make sure the medical facility, the medical team that you are taken to is versed and knowledgeable on encephalitis and AIDS dementia and AIDS medications. They should be made aware of all medications and all possible adverse reactions."

Deidre takes norvir, one of the new protease inhibitors, in capsule form. Norvir is available in liquid form, but the capsule form seems to cause less toxicity. Norvir, whose brand name is Ritonavir, must be keep refrigerated. She takes norvir with Zerit/d4T, another inhibitor. Norvir, like all other protease inhibitors, works better in combination with other inhibitors. Her experience with Crixivan was intolerance, but this drug has given her the best results so far. She started taking AZT after her first OI in 1993 after being diagnosed with cryptococcosis meningitis. From there, ddI was given, and ddC after that.

Since July 6, Deidre is more proactive in relationships. She recommends resolving conflict. "My relationship outlook has changed. You can take out the garbage a bag at a time or let it build up and get roaches, germs, bacteria and shit. My mission is to take out the garbage a bag at a time. Sometimes I do two or three bags at a time, but if you don't watch out, it will pile up, and I already have to live with AIDS. I don't have to live with roaches and rats." It brings her emotional ill health to have others cause stress and conflict. The important thing is to resolve things among those you care for. "The relationships that are constantly stressful, dump 'em. Stress unmanaged manifests itself physically and mentally for me, which leads to the emergency room." Conflict is a part of life, just like everything else. We must confront conflict as we confront everything else in life, even though confrontations of any sort can be difficult. Deidre said, "Resolving conflict, for me, eliminates a lot of unnecessary emotional stress."

Deidre's health regimen, since July, includes bench-pressing fifty pounds, walking a mile, and sometimes jogging a quarter of a mile. She's gained seven pounds since taking norvir. She eats fresh veggies and fresh fruits. More importantly, she eats what she likes. She likes to eat turnip greens, peas, snap beans, honey, cornbread, stews and pot roast. "I can't survive sucking on wafers." She has more discipline in planning her meals and taking care to sleep more. Deidre receives Social Security, so it's a hell of a sacrifice to eat right plus pay bills. Social Security is her only income. She must plan meals within a budget, as most people living with AIDS know all too well.

A typical day for Deidre starts at 6:00 A.M.: get up, eat a bowl of corn flakes and a banana, and take five norvir. By 7:00, she's taken an antacid to help stomach cramps caused by the norvir. Back to bed until 9:00, then she's up for a workout and a real breakfast of bacon, sausage, biscuits, eggs and watermelon. "Plenty of food was recommended by my nutritionist, and I don't have a problem with that, considering all the weight I've lost." Appointments, phone calls, WOMEN business, bill paying or grocery shopping until lunch. One Ensure or a strawberry SustaCal with daiquiri mix is often her midmorning treat. Lunch around 1:00 in the afternoon. Lunch is mainly a bowl of soup or a sandwich with fruit. After lunch, she spends time returning messages, seeking funding for WOMEN and making speaking engagements around the state. Often Deidre takes a short nap after lunch. "Thirty to forty-five minutes seems to recharge me." Dinner's at 6:00 and is usually big, freshly prepared by her. She takes five more norvir with her meal. She enjoys preparing her meals and cooks what she likes. "Fast food for me equals diarrhea, so I don't like eating out much."

After dinner she may eat a piece of fruit as a snack around 9:00 P.M. She listens to a tape with the sounds of the ocean, lights a scented candle, washes down in oatmeal soap and prepares her mind for a restful night's sleep. Bedtime is at 10:30, no later than 11:00. A combination of natural ways of living, lifestyle changes, and Western medications has brought Deidre back from the depths of near death.

For Deidre, HIV equaled failure. "I had been prepared my entire life, by my parents, to be beyond successful. I had been trained my entire life to be a trailblazer, a pacesetter. HIV for me meant no second chance to right that wrong. In any area I was deficient, my parents made sure I was efficient." Her family has been supportive since coming to terms with AIDS in the family.

However, their day-to-day family problems weigh so heavily on her that she finds it difficult to stay in constant contact, because she can no longer carry their problems. "I can't afford to allow them to dump the bullshit anymore. We talk and I love them dearly, but I will hang up the phone these days rather than accept problems that don't make sense." Family fighting is out of the question for her. "It's hard to unlearn my codependent nature."

Our conversation turned to the topic of minority ministers, all ministers. "As they stand in the pulpit, ministers need to incorporate AIDS and HIV into their sermons, into their litany, into their prayers," says Deidre. " If they could just do that so that it's not so taboo to say the S word (sex), not so taboo to say the A word (AIDS). God forbid, if one of them says the C word (condom) while standing in front of their congregation, they just might get ears to open. If they would say these things in a public forum in front of everybody so that people will know that it's OK to say them. Because all of them think it."

"We're all human whether we are in a pulpit or not," I told her. Ministers must harbor a spirit of openness instead of shame and guilt. Power is given when shame and guilt are used in a controlling manner. Ministers have that power over the accepting, captive congregations that listen to the "holy word." When the "holy word" is given by a minister with his or her own hidden agenda, the "holy word" becomes something other than the "Holy Word."

Quoting my dear friend: "Mr./Ms. minister, when was the last time you rolled a joint? When was the last time you had sex? When was the last time you did HIV/AIDS education? When was the last time you said that an HIV/AIDS speaker will be speaking at next Wednesday night's Bible study class? Why haven't you started a program that has speakers come in quarterly to speak about breast cancer, sickle cell anemia, hypertension? Programs such as these should educate Bible study students quarterly. The church is alive with individuals who face these and other issues seven days a week. Church is at the top of the list for a receptive, open forum of whatever religious belief, for true education on topics that affect those who sit Sunday morning fanning, singing, shouting, meditating. We can't just read parables as though they were fairy tales,

remind the congregation to put money into the offering, eat, social-
ize and then go home. How can the church fit its message into living
in the 1990s, where there are on-line services, the Internet, faxing,
beepers, cellular phones, call waiting, television viewing, microwaves,
airplanes, shuttles, elevators, movie renting, CD playing, Nintendo,
and a want-sex-now society? This is not the age of loincloths; it is
the 1990s, and AIDS is alive in our congregations. Ministers can
make a tremendous difference in the face of HIV/AIDS education,
acceptance and tolerance. There's a church on every corner in
Nashville, not to mention schools, hotels and other places of
Sunday worship.

"How many of these churches have HIV/AIDS education? How
many churches in your area have HIV/AIDS education?

"Homophobia is unacceptable. Homophobia has done more
damage to the fight against HIV/AIDS than the actual virus.
Homophobia seems inhumane. Family members that live a gay
lifestyle are seldom spoken about. Instead, families are likely to
keep it secret, show little support and alienate those who are different or who are known to have HIV/AIDS. The Bible says that
the "Word" is living and active. Have you made your message
reach phobic hearts, hearts that fear, hearts that don't trust
God?"

August 18, 1996   As this country's president celebrates his fifti-
eth birthday with much media attention in Tennessee, he takes
time to work with and listen to minority ministries who rebuild
burned-out churches.

Men over fifty are invisible in the epidemic of AIDS, in part
because of beliefs that older men do not engage in sexual behavior, that all married older men are monogamous, and that women
cannot transmit HIV to men. In addition, denial of sexual behaviors, denial of sex practices leaves open the door for the spread of
AIDS.

Education programs fall short for this sector of the population.
Education programs need to be inclusive to reach men over fifty,
men of all ages. Women are becoming infected faster. Why? In
part, because our reach has not extended to include older men.
Women are having sex with, are married to, and are having children

by older men. Sex workers (male and female) are having sex with older men. These are facts. Whether liked or disliked, these facts remain.

Bisexual men are sexually active. Gay and bisexual men over fifty are sexually active, as are their younger counterparts. Education efforts can motivate men to sustain positive behaviors in regard to sexual behavior, drug abuse and condom use. Programs do exist; more are needed. We need our men to be strong and protective of those they are in relationships with and protective of themselves. Outreach for all and more public-service announcements are definitely needed in this country.

HIV and cultural differences Sisters, wives, grandmothers, nieces and daughters are becoming infected around the world. Cultural practices contribute to increasing numbers of infections. Sexual abuse, wife inheritance, men having sex with wives' family members are only a few examples of world behaviors. The youth of the world is at risk as well. In a large number of world cultures, women are economically dependent on their partners. Safe sex is a subject that is frequently not mentioned for fear of jeopardizing everything, including life itself. Women remain at risk worldwide. HIV and poverty, HIV and isolation, HIV and STDs — these realities reach far beyond the shores of America.

Speaking on family Mother and I have suffered a great deal of damage to our desperately sought after relationship. Family acceptance is so very important. My work with HIV education has caused embarrassment for her. Her wanting me to remain silent and my inability to do so have widened the valley that has existed for years between us. Personal issues are better left unwritten, discussed only with Joan. Let's just say I've cried many tears. She's cried many tears too, I'm sure. I've suffered great losses in my relationships: my father's dying when I was twenty-three, my never feeling close to my mother. Separation between other relatives has grown as well.

A marriage of many years, a marriage with deep emotion, a marriage attached by hearts that were once one, a marriage that today has ended. Whose divorce is easy when feelings are involved, when children are involved, when mortgages are involved, when alcohol is involved, when AIDS is involved?

In many ways, life is better for the children and me. The kids are able to be kids. They don't have to worry about getting yelled at for everything they do. Loud music sometimes rocks the house. Sometimes I play it loud too. On the other side of that same coin, my T cells went up for the first time since being diagnosed, but I have an active ulcer and I've lost seven pounds. My doctor told me, "Catherine, there's more to you than HIV/AIDS."

Personal Appearance   I knew from my diagnosis in April 1994 that I would not be able to handle HIV on my own. I had to learn how to reach out and embrace the face of the Supreme Being that has been watching over my life. The goal of getting to heaven later became one of living right today, because tomorrow I truly could wake up dead. Seeking compassion in the transition from here to there is among my daily endeavors — spiritual calmness. It was through the resting of my spirit that restoration began. The light of the power I hold highest brings comfort in times of greatest need. My refusal to fall victim empowered me, thereby empowering others whose lives, I pray, will be touched, for all life will be touched in some way.

Each person facing life-changing disease masquerades many levels of loss. Therefore, in this journey I must continue to consider my children's well-being. What to do with the children when, or if, is a constant question for me. Who in my life has the morals, understanding, patience to care for them? How will they handle my future illness? Am I giving them all they need so that they will not become infected? Are they listening, or just hearing, like so many others do. I take the responsibilities of motherhood and parenting very seriously. Leaving my children with more than material wealth is a life-setting goal I continue to accomplish — thinking of what is best for them over what is best for myself, and hoping to have the fortitude to stomach the results. In addition and most important is their support. Their active participation in my work has brought them a new level of giving. Their praise and respect is often felt, even when I can't take care of them. Trusting me without conditions, my children, the extensions of myself, are clearly learning that strength is found within. I share with them often that God has given each of them all that is needed to claim their victory.

HIV becomes personal when my body reacts with an HIV-positive personality, when lymph nodes react in battle, when yeast infections ooze from my body, when fatigue keeps me away from the activities of motherhood, when myelopathy pain attacks, when I see my own blood, when the white carpet of thrush coats my tongue and gums, when I live waiting for good news from a doctor's phone call or in fear of negative news, when more tests have to run, when I have to be concerned about others' illnesses attacking me, when another opportunistic infection awaits, when HIV and hormone replacement therapy remains an anticipated frontier for positive women with hysterectomies. Further, when being placed on disability leave from my well-paying job because of unlawful medical disclosures, when discrimination is visited on me not only because of the tint of my skin but also because someone has seen me on television talking about living with HIV, when my children are cast out because their mother's reputation in the community has something to do with HIV, when friends and family excuse themselves from my life, when another friend dies of AIDS.

Though I've educated myself well and am associated with many organizations, committees, universities, and hospitals, have access to protocols, and am on what seems like thousands of mailing lists, none of this changes the fact that I am HIV-positive and progressing, much too rapidly, toward AIDS. With all the information in my possession, HIV, it seems, still has the upper hand. Human immunodeficiency virus still causes immunosuppression, which becomes AIDS. People continue to die, and still there is no *cure* — plenty of medical confusion, but no *cure*.

I have an auspicious relationship with my doctors, my pharmacy, my psychologist, my massage therapist, my spirituality, my friends, and myself. My supportive family now consists of a trusted friend, who, without children herself, has become a second mother to my children. She's taken care of me when I was facedown in disease, lifting my faith in family. She has brought more than food to my bedside; she has given when no one else has. Some friends are young and full of excitement, some are older and full of wisdom. Each adds a unique element to my life.

My father's death fifteen years past left my mother, brother, and me to carry on. My mother did not return to work after the death of her husband of thirty-six years. After his death, my mother and I settled his affairs together. Her health declined, and I was by her side, taking classes on better nutrition and care for diabetes, which she developed. With her retired and living comfortably, I felt strongly that we would always be emotionally supportive of each other.

Our family history is built in General Motors, starting with my father's migration north to a well-paying job after World War II. My brother and I were not close after we became adults. His never leaving the home we were raised in was something I couldn't relate to. My search for marriage, family, travel, and meeting life's challenges head-on was something he couldn't relate to.

In striking contrast to my friends, the reactions of my extended family have caused tremendous pain for me. I told my mother that my husband and I were both HIV-positive. After I mentioned that there was a serious problem with my blood, what was once a supportive mother (monetarily speaking) turned into nothingness. "How did this happen? What have you done?" Nothing about what she could do to help or that she loved me. The mind-set of old ways has collapsed any meaningful communication between us. She rested comfortably in her form of denial, comfortably away from me when I needed her most. Her attendance has been void during my divorce from the husband who infected me, void when opportunistic infections engulf my being. Offering to send information, giving names and telephone numbers of agencies and support groups in her town has failed to get a response. The truth seems to have fallen on deaf ears. My mother has yet to educate herself about the disease that lives in her family, within her only daughter. Keeping with that tradition, my brother reflects a mirror image of his mother. Mother does not ask about the work I do; she would rather have me keep silent so as not to bring disgrace to the family. My mother's lack of nourishment has hurt more than any other form of discrimination I have yet to face or have encountered in the past.

She knows not the opportunistic infection I battled during that very conversation. She knows not the hours of tests, agonizing days of waiting, night sweats, emergency room admissions, appetite suppression, body mass reduction, T-cell/viral load downward trends, the reality of medications, painful nights of tears, and the frequent times I literally crawl up the stairs to my bedroom because I am so weak. Nor has she read anything I've written, heard me speak, seen the video on television, read endorsements, studied files, attended any seminars, asked about travels, inquired into or read the cards that line the walls of my office from people whose lives my work has touched. Her lack of support has often left me scrambling at the last minute to find someone to stay with the children because, again, something has come up and she can't come stay with her grandchildren while I go to Washington, D.C. My mother's closed mind, closed heart and outdated way of thinking has changed my opinion of family. Though I never expected HIV to be a part of the family, I never imagined my mother's reaction being what it is. Often I wish I'd never told her. *I share this because so many women today face this disease alone. Disclosure to family members has brought so much pain to so many women.*

Releasing failed relationships has begun a cause set in motion and propelled me to push through and give life to a blossoming future full of possibilities. My desire to move forward is, in part, based on educating and giving to others what experience and knowledge I possess. Conversation with a seventeen-year-old about self-worth, HIV, morals and values encourages me to continue. The blessing is that this promising minority youth listened and now reads, educates herself, and insists that her partner use protection when engaging in sexual activities. However small an influence I've been, she now speaks of a future full of possibilities, not a future with HIV/AIDS.

I encourage those closest to me to get tested, eliminating doubt, because friends think of themselves when looking at me. I have shared with close friends their days of waiting for results of an HIV test. While emotions run the full gamut, they bring memories of past behaviors, failed marriages, drug use, sexual violations, years of forgotten moments in time. Reflection can be difficult, but my friends know that they are better off knowing. The decision to be tested and the experience of being tested are difficult, I know, but who today has the right not to be tested?

Somehow, fault and blame become more than the issues of disease. The stigma of being a woman, black, mother, infected, inferior takes over any reasoning of what can be done to help live a quality life. Our minority families extend little support, our minority religious leaders honor silence and our black brothers and sisters die alone. No honor is found in abandonment. No crown can be worn for those who believe themselves better or untouched. Women — minority women, especially — face an imprisonment of isolation thrust on us by society and members of our own family. I, an African American, am disproportionately affected by AIDS. I represent the fastest growing group of HIV infections in the United States and abroad. Minority women are 56 percent of all AIDS cases; 21 percent are Hispanic women. The women represented tend to be poor, young, and from disenfranchised communities in inner-city neighborhoods. However, in 1996–97, soccer moms' rates of infection are no laughing matter. Forty-two percent of the 21 million adults living with HIV/AIDS worldwide are women.

The epidemiology and clinical presentation of women with AIDS deserve special attention, because of our unique role in childbearing, child care, transmission, sexual makeup, and differences in clinical problems from those of men. Every three minutes, another person becomes infected. Every day, another dies of an AIDS-related illness. How I, or others, become or became infected is irrelevant in the face of disease.

Because my reality is HIV, it does not negate the concern I feel for others facing breast cancer, mental illness, abuse, abandonment and forced societal judgment. I stand not in judgment but in the light of hope — hope that women will become aware of the power they hold. For me, a *cure* is found in the human compassion that makes the world aware that all humankind is either infected or affected. Mine is one of many personal appearance experiences.

August 23, 1996   Protocol is a term given to studies conducted by clinics, hospitals and laboratories that study the effectiveness of a drug — sometimes referred to as clinical trials. Out of these studies or clinical trials that are conducted throughout the United States and around the world come drugs. These new drugs are called protease inhibitors. One is called Crixivan, one is called norvir and the third is called Invirase or Saquinavir. More are under study and soon to come.

Anyone who is taking one of these protease inhibitors must understand the drug. The effects of drug doses, mixing over-the-counter medication, and food intake are vitally important. These protease inhibitors should be taken at prescribed dose levels, and not missing doses is very important too.

Ask questions when told about starting on protease inhibitors or any other drugs. We as women cannot be afraid to ask questions of our health care team. We are the star quarterbacks of our health care team. We deserve to ask questions, we deserve clear, understandable answers.

Viral load testing is a test whereby blood is drawn at a clinic, doctor's office, hospital or lab. Viral load is the measured amount of HIV in the blood. Viral load testing is beginning to show good results, and this test has been approved by the Food and Drug Administration. According to the International AIDS Society, people should get two baseline tests taken two to four weeks apart. Again, ask questions. Have the health care team explain clearly what viral load testing will be used for and what determining the results will mean personally. Someone whose viral load is undetectable does not mean they have no more HIV in the blood or body tissue. It means that the amount of measurable HIV found in the blood is low. Low means 10,000 copies/mm or less.

Again, all protease inhibitors should be taken as prescribed. Keeping communications open with your health care team is very important.

I understand the pain and fear. I know what it is like to hide and feel alone after being diagnosed HIV-positive. I know what it is like to have no one to talk to. I understand how difficult it is to come to terms with this disease. I would like to reach as many men, women and children as possible to let them know that they are not alone. WOMEN is a small grassroots outreach HIV/AIDS organization that advocates for women and families. We work in the community, and we are your community. Through shared knowledge, women can become empowered. Through shared sisterhood, we can all work together for the betterment of women and families.

Whether infected by HIV/AIDS or affected by HIV/AIDS, we as people are all touched by the virus that causes AIDS.

Some of the information may be foreign. Protease inhibitors? Clinical trials? What medications to take? When to take medications? Should this medication be taken with the other medications I am on? Knowing that others in the community face some of these same concerns has a way of easing the stress, in turn allowing that feeling of isolation to be replaced with knowledge. You are not alone. ■

■ Afterword ■

Ian Mayo-Smith

Why should it happen to her? A respectable, middle-class woman living in a pleasant suburb of Nashville with a good, steady job at a manufacturing plant. Why should her life be turned upside down? Why should she have to be infected with HIV? If you believe that there is a purpose in life, if you believe in a loving God, it doesn't seem to make sense that Catherine Wyatt-Morley should become infected with HIV; it doesn't seem fair that her three children, Brandon, Aaron and Jalyon, should have their lives affected by their parents' illness.

But then you look at the life of Catherine and her children since that horrifying day when she learned that she was infected. I suspect that Catherine must always have had leadership qualities. Look at how those qualities have been used since that painful discovery. Catherine has used her own pain, both physical and psychological, to help others — to help others to understand, to help others so that they will avoid contracting the disease, to bring comfort to others who are infected with or affected by this virus.

It was through our mutual friends George and Bernice Lemon, a retired doctor and a retired nurse, that I came to meet Catherine. Berni had met Catherine at the dentist's office and had struck up a friendship with her. George and Berni are deeply caring people and people of deep faith. Catherine obviously felt very comfortable with Berni and told her story to her. She mentioned that she was putting together a book based on letters she had started writing to her children after she learned that she had HIV. Berni

IAN MAYO-SMITH is an emeritus professor at the University of Connecticut and former director of the Institute of Public Service International at the university. He is also vice president of Kumarian Press and the author of a number of books.

suggested that she send the manuscript to me at Kumarian Press and mention that they had recommended that she do so.

So one day I went into my office at KP and found a large box on my desk. It contained the manuscript, cover letters, supporting materials and a videotape. I took the videotape home and watched it. It was moving. Later that day, I showed it to my wife, Krishna Sondhi, who is president of KP; she too found it moving.

Later I flew down to Nashville to meet Catherine. My friends George and Berni put me up in their home while I was there. Upon meeting Catherine, I was amazed how this woman who had suffered so much could be so full of laughter and good humor. I enjoyed every minute I spent with her and her family and felt uplifted and invigorated from simply being with them.

One evening, George, Berni and I were over at the Morley home for the evening meal. Jalyon gave George, Berni and me each a small packet, a present. Inside was a small color picture of her and a penny. Jalyon told us that we should put the penny in the window when we went to bed and make sure that Lincoln's head was the right way up. Then we were to make a wish. She told us that the wish would go up to God, and He would send us something back.

Well, I don't believe that you should ever underestimate the wisdom of a ten-year-old child, so I did as she had said. The next day, during my early morning meditation, a fable came into my mind, and I wrote it down. It was a kind of parable about the Morley family. That evening, when the Morleys and the Lemons and I were having dinner at a local restaurant, I told Jalyon, "The penny worked," and I read the fable to them at the table. Here it is.

The Rose Garden

There was once a great gardener. He planted a great garden of rose trees and he tended all of those trees. When the weather was dry he watered them and he would put fertilizer around the base of the trees.

But there was one tree that was very special to him because he knew that this tree would produce exceptionally beautiful and sweet smelling roses. So he used to put extra large amounts of organic manure on this tree.

Now the tree hated to have all this dirty stinking stuff put on it and the tree protested and said to the gardener, whose name was God, "It's not fair. Why do you have to keep heaping this shit on me?"

The tree could not hear what God said in reply because the wind was whistling through the leaves. In fact, the tree wasn't sure that God was listening to what it said.

But God kept on nurturing the tree, though to the tree it didn't feel much like nurturing.

And then one day God came along with his pruning shears and he pruned off a big branch of the tree and it hurt like hell. And the tree cried and called out to God, "Why'd you have to do that?"

And God said, "I am so sorry. I did not want to do that, but that branch was affected by a blight and if I hadn't pruned that branch the blight might have destroyed the whole tree."

And in spite of everything the tree grew strong and healthy and, just as God had planned, it produced four of the most beautiful blossoms in the whole of the garden, and people would come and stop by this tree to see the roses and smell their perfume.

But it was funny, there were some people who just could not see the beauty and relish the fragrance of the roses. All they noticed were the thorns on the rose tree and they said, "Just look at those dreadful thorns. I hate trees like that." And you had to feel pity for such people because of what they were missing.

But God called his family and friends to come and see and enjoy the roses. And some took pictures of these roses to show to others. And some wrote about them so that others could grow beautiful healthy roses too.

And one of God's friends said to God, "These are very special roses. Do you have a name for them?"

And God said, "Yes, I have a name for each of the four blossoms on this tree. That big pink rose in the center of the tree— that's my Catherine rose. And those two strong, deep red roses, they're called Brandon and Aaron. And that beautiful yellow rose that looks like it's smiling at you, that's my Jalyon rose."

And the world was a little bit better and a little bit sweeter and a little bit kinder because of this special rose tree. ■

■ Appendix 1 ■
Some Statistics on
HIV/AIDS and STDs

- Every hour, two to four Americans under the age of twenty become infected with HIV.

- By June 1995, 2,184 children between the ages of thirteen and nineteen had been diagnosed with AIDS.

- Every year, over three million teenagers are infected with some form of STD.

- Current studies show that the average age of first-time sexual experiences among American teenagers is sixteen; more than 54 percent are students in grades nine through twelve. What about the children who are as young as ten who are sexually active? The report didn't show those results.

- A startling 17,745 AIDS cases were reported in the adult population aged twenty to twenty-four.

- Between twenty-seven and fifty-four children are infected with HIV each and every day due to unprotected sex and sex with multiple partners.

- In 1990, almost two-thirds of the reported STD cases were in persons under the age of twenty-five. Twelve million STD cases were reported that year. How many were not reported? ■

Information obtained from Centers for Disease Control and Prevention and National AIDS Policy reports.

■ Appendix 2 ■
Fact and Fiction about HIV and AIDS

Facts:

- Staying in control protects you against HIV/AIDS.
- Practicing abstinence protects you against HIV/AIDS.
- Refusing to share needles with anyone protects you against HIV/AIDS.
- Refusing to have unprotected sex (whether anal, vaginal or oral) gives you some protection against HIV/AIDS, although condoms by no means give total protection.

You do not get infected by:

- donating blood
- touching or hugging someone who is HIV-positive or has AIDS
- shaking hands with someone who is HIV-positive or has AIDS
- eating food prepared by a person who is HIV-positive or has AIDS
- social or dry kissing someone who is HIV-positive or has AIDS
- sneezes or coughs from someone who is HIV-positive or has AIDS
- sharing toilet seats, showers or bathrooms with someone who is HIV-positive or has AIDS
- working with someone who is HIV-positive or has AIDS
- using swimming pools or hot tubs with someone who is HIV-positive or has AIDS
- using clean drinking glasses or dishes that have been used by someone who is HIV-positive or has AIDS

- riding public transportation used by someone who is HIV-positive or has AIDS
- sharing books or magazines with an HIV-positive person or a person with AIDS
- being bitten by mosquitoes or other bugs

You do get infected by contact with the bodily fluids of an infected person. The most common way this happens is through sex, both heterosexual and homosexual. ■

▪ Appendix 3 ▪
Resources

Magazines

Positively Aware   The bimonthly journal of Test Positive Aware Network in Chicago. Focus is on treatment and social and personal issues related to living with HIV. $15 donation requested for six issues. 258 W. Belmont Ave., Chicago, IL 60657; (312) 472-6397.

POZ   A lifestyle magazine for people affected by HIV. $19.95; free for those with HIV. Old Chelsea Station, Box 1279, New York, NY 10113-1279; (212) 242-1900.

Seasons   Newsletter of the National Native American AIDS Prevention Center. Free subscriptions in the United States. American AIDS Prevention Center, 3515 Grand Ave., Suite 100, Oakland, CA 94610-2011; (510) 444-2051.

Books

And the Band Played On: Politics, People, and the AIDS Epidemic. Randy Shilts. Penguin USA. (See also under videotapes.)

Days of Grace: A Memoir. Arthur Ashe. Ballantyne Books.

The Essential HIV Treatment Fact Book. Laura Pinsky et al. Pocket Books.

HIV & AIDS: The Global Interconnection. Edited by Elizabeth Reid. Kumarian Press.

My Name Is Mary: A Memoir. Mary Fisher. Scribner's.

My Own Country: A Doctor's Story. Abraham Verghese. Vintage Books.

Sarah's Song: A True Story of Love and Courage. Janice A. Burns. Warner Books.

Seasons of Grief and Grace: A Sister's Story of AIDS. Susan Ford Wiltshire. Vanderbilt University Press.

Videotapes

And the Band Played On Available from most video stores.

Reasons to Live: Women, Their Families and HIV Produced by Catherine Wyatt-Morley. This video features a number of the people mentioned in this book. Available from WOMEN, 1113 Murfreesboro Rd., Suite 106-301, Franklin, TN 37064.

Philadelphia With Tom Hanks and Antonio Banderas. Available from most video stores.

The World Wide Web and the Internet

An enormous amount of information on HIV and AIDS is available on the World Wide Web and on on-line services such as America Online, Compuserve and Prodigy. No detailed list is given here, as the information is constantly being updated. ▪

▪ Glossary ▪
Acronyms and Technical Terms

ACTG	AIDS Clinical Trial Group
ACTG 076	protocol 076, mandating HIV testing of pregnant women
ACT-UP	AIDS Coalition to Unleash Power
AIDS	acquired immunodeficiency syndrome
AZT	the first of the drugs developed to combat AIDS, also known as Retrovir, zidovudine or ZDV
CAT scan	computerized axial tomography
CCC (3Cs)	Comprehensive Care Clinic
CCG	Community Constituency Group
CDC	Centers for Disease Control and Prevention
CD4	indicator of white blood cells killed or disabled during HIV infection
clinical trial	study testing the effectiveness of a drug or vaccine given to humans
CMV	cytomegalovirus, herpes virus, which commonly causes opportunistic diseases in persons with AIDS and others with immune suppression
CMV retinitis	an eye disease
ddC	dideoxycytidine or zalcitabine, a drug that inhibits HIV replication
ddI	dideoxyinosine, didanosine or Videx, a drug that inhibits HIV replication
dementia	chronic intellectual impairment
DNA	molecular chain found in genes within the nucleus of each cell
d4T	Staduvine or Zerit, a dideoxynucleoside that inhibits HIV replication

EEG	electroencephalogram
EES	erythromycin ethylsuccinate
ELISA	enzyme-linked immunosorbent assay, a test to determine the presence of HIV anitibodies in the blood
FDA	Food and Drug Administration
HIV	human immunodeficiency virus
ICU	intensive care unit
IV	intravenous
MAC	*Mycobacterium avium* complex, a common opportunistic infection caused by two similar mycobacterial organisms, *Mycobacterium avium* and *Mycobacterium intracellulare*
MRI	magnetic resonance imaging
NA	Narcotics Anonymous
OI	opportunistic infection
PI	principal investigator
PNI	psychoneuroimmunology
protease inhibitors	drugs that inhibit the replicative life cycle of HIV
Ryan White Care Act	the 1990 act representing the largest dollar investment made by Congress in the fight against HIV/AIDS
STD	sexually transmitted disease
TB	tuberculosis
T cell or T lymphocyte	white blood cells of the body
3TC	also known as lamivudine, a drug that inhibits HIV replication through viral DNA; normally used in conjunction with AZT
viral load	the amount of HIV found in the blood
wasting syndrome	involuntary loss of 10 percent of baseline body weight
Western blot	a laboratory tests for HIV antibodies; it is more accurate than ELISA
WOMEN	Women on Maintaining Education and Nutrition, a grassroots nonprofit organization serving both rural and urban populations
WORTH	Women on Reasons to Heal, an HIV support group

 Kumarian Press is dedicated to publishing and distributing books and other media that will have a positive social and economic impact on the lives of peoples living in "Third World" conditions no matter where they live.

As well as books on International Health, Kumarian Press also publishes books on Peace and Conflict Resolution, the Environment, International Development, Nongovernmental Organizations, Government, Gender and Development

To receive a complimentary catalog, request writer's guidelines, or to order books, call or write:

Kumarian Press, Inc.
14 Oakwood Avenue
West Hartford, CT 06119-2127
USA

Inquiries: 860-233-5895
Fax: 860-233-6072
Order toll free: 800-289-2664

e-mail: kpbooks@aol.com